GOD'S SERVANTS, THE PROPHETS

Smyth & Helwys Publishing, Inc.
6316 Peake Road
Macon, Georgia 31210-3960
1-800-747-3016
©2014 by Smyth & Helwys Publishing
All rights reserved.
Printed in the United States of America.

The paper used in this publication meets the minimum requirements of
American National Standard for Information Sciences—
Permanence of Paper for Printed Library Materials.
ANSI Z39.48–1984. (alk. paper)

Library of Congress Cataloging-in-Publication Data

Bibb, Bryan D.
God's servants, the prophets / by Bryan D. Bibb.
pages cm
ISBN 978-1-57312-758-5 (pbk. : alk. paper)
1. Bible. Prophets--Introductions. I. Title.
BS1505.52.B53 2015
224'.06--dc23

2014045301

God's Servants, the Prophets

Bryan D. Bibb

Contents

Acknowledgements	vii
Introduction **Who Were the Prophets?**	1
Chapter 1 **Amos**	29
Chapter 2 **Hosea**	53
Chapter 3 **Isaiah**	71
Chapter 4 **Micah**	103
Chapter 5 **Zephaniah**	115
Chapter 6 **Nahum**	121
Chapter 7 **Habakkuk**	131
Chapter 8 **Jeremiah/Lamentations**	143
Chapter 9 **Obadiah**	175
Chapter 10 **Conclusion**	181

Acknowledgements

This book from Smyth & Helwys is part of a series titled "All the Bible" and covers preexilic prophetic literature. Information about exilic and postexilic prophets can be found in the companion volume by Wayne Ballard, *Exile and Beyond*. Also, interested readers are invited to visit my website, bryanbibb.com, for discussion of the larger prophetic tradition as well as for updates and additional material related to the book.

I would like to express my heartfelt appreciation to Keith Gammons and to Smyth & Helwys for the opportunity to write this volume and for their extraordinary patience in its preparation.

I am grateful for my excellent colleagues at Furman University who have supported me through seasons of joy and sorrow. I would like to give a special thanks to John Shelley and David Rutledge, who are retiring after many years of diligent and faithful service to the religion department, and to new friend and colleague Tim Wardle, who was generous with his time and insights in the final editing process. Thank you to my students who have been lively conversation partners over the years. I am more grateful than words can express for the love and support of my wife, Jennifer, and our boys, Joseph and Nolan.

Finally, this book is dedicated to my mother, Dorothy Bibb Hardy, the person who first taught me the importance of a thoughtful faith. She inspired me with her hard work in health and with her tenacity in illness. She loved fiercely and lived bravely. As was said of Ruth, she was a woman of valor.

Introduction

Who Were the Prophets?

The central subject of this book is the Israelite and Judean prophetic literature from the preexilic period. Prophetic activity is attested from the earliest stages of the national history of Israel and continued until it was phased out in the Persian and Greek periods in favor of priestly authority, Torah study, and—in some circles—apocalyptic reflection. This chapter will first examine the basic character of the prophetic literature in the Bible and then suggest the most important questions we should bring to our study of the prophets who ministered in Israel and Judah from the eighth to the sixth century BCE.

Many definitions have been advanced for the biblical prophets, all relating in some way to their distinctive relationship between God and the people. For example, here are a few terms that have been used to describe the prophets' task:

- Ecstatic Revealer: one who proclaims mysterious truths while in the grip of an emotional, rapturous spell. May work alone or as part of a prophetic "guild."
- Messianic Predictor: one who reveals the future coming of God's anointed one, the Messiah.
- Religious Genius: a charismatic leader who understands the inner workings of Israel's religious and theological traditions and teaches them to the people.

- Political Functionary: one who works in the service of the king to predict the success or failure of royal decisions, especially military actions.

While each of these definitions conveys a specific function or role of the biblical prophets, in the Bible the most important role of a prophet is that of "messenger," one who is commissioned to deliver messages from Yahweh, the divine king, to the human king and to his subjects. In fact, the most common phrase in the prophetic literature is "Thus says the LORD" ("LORD" is the standard English rendering of the divine name *Yahweh*). So when the prophet speaks, he begins by saying "Thus says Yahweh," indicating that the prophet delivers a specific message from God to the listeners. The prophets claim sometimes that they have seen God and heard God's voice and that they have intimate knowledge of divine plans. The nature of these revelatory experiences is, however, not as important as the fact that the words are *from* God. The so-called "false prophets" use the same introductory phrase, so listeners cannot base their reception of the prophecy only on the language used. Even so, delivering a message from God is the central requirement for being a prophet.

What kind of message did they deliver, and what forms did it take? The simplest unit of prophecy is called an "oracle," which can be as short as one verse and as long as several chapters strung together. Often, however, several related oracles are grouped together into a larger unit, which can make it difficult to identify each oracle and understand how it is connected to those surrounding it. Moreover, it is common to see individual oracles augmented with explanatory phrases or supplemented with additional verses from a later time period. The term "form criticism" describes attempts to identify the "original" oracle behind the complex final form of a prophetic text. Although this book will not address much of that work, we will notice texts in which editorial additions have subtly altered the meaning of the original.

The most characteristic type of oracle is the "judgment oracle," which pronounces God's judgment on a guilty person or group. The usual analogy is that of a courtroom. A judgment

INTRODUCTION

oracle begins with a list of the sins and offenses of the guilty party, or an indictment. Usually signaled by a resounding "therefore," the oracle then presents the punishment for those sins, or the sentencing phase of the trial. The point of a judgment oracle is not merely to tell the future, but to justify what God is doing or is about to do. In fact, most punishments described by the prophets are either ongoing or about to occur. Judgment oracles provide an explanation of these events so the people will know who is responsible (God) and the divine purpose behind it.

In addition to the judgment oracle, the prophets use "forms" such as salvation oracles, oracles against the nations (a special type of judgment oracle addressed to foreign powers), prophetic reports (stories about things that happen to the prophets or things they do), and various kinds of narratives, hymns, and allegories. Readers of the prophets should start by identifying which verses make up an oracle and what kind of oracle it is. Noticing the difference between judgment and salvation oracles is a basic first step in the interpretation process.

The prophets deliver their oracles in a variety of social settings. One common role for a prophet in the ancient Near East is as a source of information for the king. Consider the story of Micaiah ben Imlah in 1 Kings 22, in which King Ahab makes use of a stable of prophets (including Micaiah) to predict the success or failure of his military campaigns. Isaiah and Jeremiah both deliver oracles directly to the king of Judah and enjoy a high level of access to the royal ear. Other prophets, however, seem more "peripheral," meaning that they do not have social or political status. These prophets wander among towns and deliver messages from God in an informal setting, sometimes standing in a public square. Readers should pay attention to the social setting of a prophetic oracle (e.g., where it is given, who is in the audience, and so on). Such information helps readers know what the oracle is intended to accomplish and to whom the message is being sent.

One common approach to studying the prophets is to explore the prophets' personal histories and actions. There is indeed some information about the individual prophets recorded in the books that bear their names. For example, Amos 7 tells a story about Amos's conflict with a priest named Amaziah. Isaiah's family life plays a role in his oracles in Isaiah 7–8, as his sons become "signs" of God's future actions. Hosea uses his personal life (marriage to a promiscuous woman) as an illustration for the prophetic message. Jeremiah's dealings with temple and palace officials and his actions during the destruction of Jerusalem by the Babylonians appear throughout the book of Jeremiah. One must remember, however, that the personal information given about the prophets is intended to support the message itself. In the chapters that follow, we will not attempt to reconstruct biographies of the prophets, but place the emphasis where it belongs: on the oracles within their literary context. The personal stories found throughout these books are part of this literary context.

Prophetic Words and Texts

The prophetic literature in the Hebrew Bible includes some of the most familiar texts in the Bible, but they are also some of the most obscure and difficult texts to understand. Readers of the New Testament, for example, encounter several prophetic passages that have become central affirmations of the Christian tradition. Individual verses have taken on a life of their own: "A virgin shall conceive and bear a son, and shall call his name Emmanuel"; "A voice was heard in Ramah, wailing and loud lamentation, Rachel weeping for her children"; "The spirit of the LORD is upon me, because he has anointed me to bring good news to the poor"; "Everyone who calls on the name of the LORD shall be saved"; "The righteous shall live by faith." Each of these verses can be found within the prophetic texts discussed in this book.

It is important to remember, however, that these individual verses were never meant to stand on their own. They are each part of a larger "oracle" that was spoken or written by a prophet at a particular time and place in history. While these words may be familiar, all too often we do not have the needed historical and literary context to interpret them fully and

Introduction

properly. Also, the great majority of prophetic literature does not enjoy this level of familiarity.

It is safe to say that, taken as a whole, the prophets are one of the more neglected sections of the Bible. There are three major obstacles to reading and understanding the prophets well. First, once we try to understand a whole oracle rather than a few words or phrases out of context, we are faced with the difficulty of identifying and analyzing the historical context of the passage. Many oracles provide clues to their historical context by saying who was king at the time or referring to other historical events such as invasions and natural disasters. These references were intended for the scribal scholars who created and studied these texts, and we often do not have the historical knowledge we needed to decipher them. Moreover, each of the prophetic books has been edited and augmented by later prophets and scribes. It is not clear, for instance, that all of the oracles in Amos date to the time of Amos himself. Thus, the essential work of historical contextualizing can be difficult and uncertain. Despite these difficulties, a basic understanding of the prophets as historical figures and historical books is well within the reach of non-expert interpreters.

The second major obstacle to understanding the prophets is that the literature itself is difficult. Most of it is poetry and employs poetic techniques such as the use of metaphor and imagery, unusual or incomplete grammatical constructions, and ambiguous speeches. As poetry, it must be read slowly and aloud for the full effect, which is not how people today are inclined to read. Later in this chapter, and in each chapter of the book, we will describe the key literary features of the prophetic literature so it may become less strange or difficult. Also, readers would do well to consult two or three different translations, ideally ones that take different approaches to the metaphorical elements of the original Hebrew text. The King James Version is beautiful and classic; the English Standard Version is highly "literal" and wooden-sounding; The Message is extremely "dynamic"; others, such as the New International Version and the Common English Bible, are somewhere in the middle. None of these is "right" or "wrong" in the way it translates a prophetic passage. Rather, each emphasizes different aspects of the text, and readers can benefit from comparing and contrasting these versions. An excellent resource for comparing translations is the website biblegateway.com, which has many translations freely available and even allows one to open multiple translations in parallel for comparison. All translations in this book, unless otherwise noted, come from the New Revised Standard Version.

The third major obstacle in reading the prophets is the modern tendency to isolate individual verses and interpret them as if they can be applied directly, out of context, to events that happened centuries later. Readers often assume that the prophets were primarily future-predictors who speak in cryptic language to future generations and that particular words and phrases have "secret" or "hidden" meanings that can only be unlocked by a skilled expert. However, the prophets spoke first and foremost to their own communities about events facing them in their present and near future. Prophetic oracles were delivered as authentic words in their time and place, drawing upon their audiences' knowledge and concerns and explaining God's intentions in their world. These words find significance and meaning for later readers, but readers should learn first about the prophet's world, about the profound issues they faced, and about the theological traditions upon which they drew. In this way one may understand the prophetic oracles as whole and coherent speeches, as they were originally understood. This approach respects the prophetic oracles for what they are rather than imposing any external set of assumptions and methods on them. In the "Theological Traditions" section below, and in each chapter of the book, we will begin to understand the prophets as divine messengers in their own time and place and with an enduring message for all generations.

Introduction

Historical Context

A good understanding of Israel's history is crucial for one to understand the prophets well. These prophetic texts were spoken, written, edited, and experienced in the midst of real historical circumstances that were constantly shifting. Indeed, once we read beyond the level of single-verse quotations and begin to read whole paragraphs or chapters, we immediately encounter specific historical references and situations. This can be a frustrating experience unless one has grasped the basic outline of Israelite history and has access to more detailed information.

For instance, one of the most famous sentences in prophetic literature is found in Isaiah 7:14, which the King James Version renders as "a virgin shall conceive, and bear a son, and shall call his name Immanuel." That verse is quoted by the Gospel of Matthew in its description of Mary's miraculous virginal conception: "Now all this was done, that it might be fulfilled which was spoken of the Lord by the prophet, saying, Behold, a virgin shall be with child, and shall bring forth a son, and they shall call his name Emmanuel, which being interpreted is, God with us" (Matt 1:22-23 KJV).

Once we read the sentences and paragraphs immediately before and after this verse, however, we encounter possibly confusing references to Ahaz and Assyria, Ephraim and Aram, kings named Rezin and Pekah, etc. There is also the promise that something momentous will happen before this child learns how to eat curds (Isa 7:15).

If we would like to understand this prophecy, we must give some attention to its historical context. Who are these kings, and in what kinds of international struggles were they involved? How did these events affect Judah, and how did this prophecy comfort or challenge Isaiah's listener (i.e., King Ahaz) at this moment in time? There is a rich historical context lying behind the child Immanuel that is integral to its interpretation. Certainly, we may also consider how Matthew interpreted the prophecy and how it became one of the central Christian prophecies in the Bible, but we must first understand what this meant in Isaiah's own time. For more on that question, see the section on "The Prophets and the New Testament" in the last chapter of this book.

It is recommended that all readers have access to a brief introduction to Israelite history and perhaps a Bible dictionary. It would also be good to have a study Bible, such as *The Access Study Bible* from Oxford, open with you as you read this book. Not only will this let you read the texts under discussion, but the maps and notes will also be helpful. It is often surprising how important geography is to the development of literature and theology.

Three Moments in Time

Each of the chapters in this book will begin with some discussion of historical context. By way of introduction, it is helpful to think about the long and complex history of Israel in terms of "three key moments." Donald Gowan organizes his excellent introduction to prophetic theology around these three key turning points: the destruction of the northern kingdom of Israel by the Assyrians in 722 BCE, the destruction of the southern kingdom of Judah by the Babylonians in 586 BCE, and the restoration of Judah's religious institutions by the Persians in 538 BCE.[1] Each of the prophetic texts can be understood in its relation to these three moments: either leading up to, living in the midst of, or reflecting upon these events.

Timeline

These dates are presented as "working facts" to help us keep events in their relative order. Much historical debate surrounds each of these events, both in terms of the dating as well as the nature of the events themselves. The earlier periods are not significant for dating the prophetic texts; however, they are presented here to give the reader a sense of how much time passes between key historical moments in the history of Israel and Judah.

Introduction

There are two important facts to keep in mind with regard to this timeline. First, most prophetic activity clusters around the three dates of 722, 586, and 538. After the establishment of the Torah as the normative rule for the community,

1250 BCE	Moses and the exodus
1000 BCE	David establishes the united monarchy
928 BCE	Solomon dies; monarchy splits into north (Israel) and south (Judah)
722 BCE	Assyria destroys Israel and makes Judah its vassal
587–586 BCE	Babylon destroys Judah; beginning of Babylonian exile
538 BCE	Cyrus, king of Persia, defeats Babylon and begins restoration period
515 BCE	The temple is rebuilt in Jerusalem
450 BCE	Ezra establishes the Torah as normative law
336 BCE	Alexander the Great; beginning of Greek Hellenistic period
167–164 BCE	Maccabean revolt
63 BCE	Pompey establishes Roman control of Judah
27–30 CE	Jesus of Nazareth's public ministry

administered in Jerusalem by a priestly class and Persian-appointed governors, prophetic activity largely ceased.

Second, New Testament texts that quote the prophets were written anywhere from 500 to 800 years later than their source material. The historical and theological context of early Christianity is totally different from that of ancient Israel. Interpreters who are familiar with the prophets primarily through the lens of New Testament quotation may initially find it disorienting to read the prophets within their own historical context. The central claim of this book, however, is that such historical reading is essential to understanding the prophets and will ultimately enrich one's understanding of the New Testament authors' use of prophetic material. There is more discussion about Christian interpretation of the prophets in the conclusion chapter.

Israel

After the 200-year period of settlement and organization that followed the exodus, Israel created a monarchical system similar to its neighbors. The first king, Saul, ruled a small area in the northern hills surrounding the valley of Jezreel. The upstart David, after a period of mercenary service to the Philistines, established a rival kingdom in the southern region of Hebron. After Saul's death David unified those two kingdoms into one and moved his capital to the newly captured city of Jerusalem. He and his son Solomon continued to consolidate and expand the united kingdom, but upon Solomon's death the two regions reverted to their former separation, with the northern kingdom keeping the name "Israel" and the Davidic southern kingdom "Judah."

This division began the period knows as the "divided monarchy." The northern kingdom of Israel was, for most of its history, the more powerful and important kingdom. It is during the ninth century BCE that we find the important early prophets (Elijah and Elisha) and during the 8th century BCE the first two "writing prophets" (Amos and Hosea).

In the second half of the eighth century BCE, the great empire of Assyria began a period of westward expansion that eventually toppled a series of nations, including Israel and eventually Egypt. Most of the prophecies in Amos come from the time period just before Assyria's invasion, and Hosea seems to be a bit later, covering the years of the invasion and eventual conquering of Samaria in 722 BCE.

Due to its geographical position in the Judean hills, Jerusalem was not in the direct path of Assyria's conquests.

Introduction

Judah's kings (Ahaz and Hezekiah, most notably) were given the option of becoming "vassals," independent states under the ultimate political and military control of the Assyrian Empire. Two prophets were on the scene in Judah during the eighth century, Isaiah and Micah, and they provide fascinating perspectives on how the destruction of Israel was perceived by its southern neighbor. After 722 BCE Israel as a political entity ceased to exist outside of the theological imagination of later Judeans.

Judah

All prophetic texts after Amos and Hosea come from the southern kingdom of Judah. The eighth-century prophets Isaiah and Micah attempt to explain how the destruction of Israel and the sparing of Judah by Assyria are part of God's larger plan. They establish the key elements of "Zion theology," which expresses God's unique commitment to Jerusalem as the place where God chooses to dwell and where God's chosen ruler—the Davidic king—will reign forever. The tragic destruction of Israel, however, served as a powerful reminder that the people of Judah should not take God's protection for granted. Although it was God's desire that Judah survive the crisis, the establishment of Assyrian domination was seen as God's plan to discipline Judah, stopping short of its destruction. Thus, historical events of the eighth century BCE influenced not only Judah's political future, but also the development of its theology.

In the last half of the seventh century BCE, Assyrian domination began to wane in the region as the empire had to address crumbling political control closer to home. The Judean king Josiah seized this moment to establish some measure of independence from Assyria, as reflected in his religious reforms in 2 Kings 22–23. As Assyrian power receded, however, the gap was soon filled by the reemergent Babylonian Empire. Perhaps the most crucial turning point was the battle of Carchemish in 605 BCE, which the Assyrians technically won, because it marked the last time Assyria was able to muster any kind of defense against Babylonian encroachment on its empire.

Five prophets emerged during the last quarter of the seventh century BCE: Zephaniah, Jeremiah, Nahum, Habakkuk, and Obadiah. At first, the downfall of the Assyrian Empire was greeted with malicious glee by the Judeans, as reflected in the prophecy of Nahum, which describes in loving detail the violent downfall of Nineveh in 612 BCE. Likewise, Zephaniah includes an oracle against Assyria, predicting its complete downfall as a result of its arrogance (Zeph 2:13-15).

It soon became clear, however, that the Assyrian threat was being replaced by another just as bad, if not worse. The prophecies of Habakkuk and Jeremiah predict the kingdom of Judah will suffer violent defeat at the hands of the Babylonians, but both texts find this notion unsettling. Habakkuk in particular questions the justice of God in choosing such a violent enemy to accomplish the divine purpose (Hab 1:12–2:1). Jeremiah's prophecy extends from before the Babylonian takeover, through the tumultuous decades of Babylonian control of Judah, to the final destruction of Jerusalem by Nebuchadnezzar in 586 BCE. The narratives and prophecies of Jeremiah, as well as the tiny book of Obadiah, provide a fascinating and troubling picture of Jerusalem's distress and its leaders' inability to avoid the impending disaster.

The beginning of the Babylonian exile is dated to 586 BCE, though the larger diaspora began under the Assyrians in the eighth century and had taken its first major toll on the kingdom of Judah in 597 BCE. When Jerusalem and the temple were burned, the king of Judah murdered, and many of the people forcibly taken to the foreign land of Babylon, a major reevaluation of Israel and Judah's history, identity, values, and future prospects took place. Prophetic texts from Amos all the way through Jeremiah were collected and edited for the purpose of explaining to the people why such misfortune had befallen them and where their future hope might be found. No single event is as important as the exile in the creation of the Bible and of early Judaism.

Introduction

Yehud

The final "moment" in Israel's history falls outside the scope of this book. In 538 BCE the Babylonian Empire dissolved with a whimper as the Persian conqueror Cyrus the Great assumed control over the city of Babylon. Among other notable changes in imperial policy, Cyrus decreed that people-groups that had been displaced by the Babylonians could repatriate to their ancestral homes. Some Judeans living in Babylon and elsewhere traveled "home" to Jerusalem to rebuild their society. The Judeans were not given political independence, but the Persians encouraged local populations to develop and promote their own religious identity and religious law codes. The Persians funded the rebuilding of the temple, which was rededicated in 515 BCE.

During and after the exile, Judeans (now "Yehud," a province of the Persian Empire) began to think of themselves again as "Israel" and began to develop a religious identity not tied to their political structure. With a local hierarchy composed of priests, a temple as cultural and religious center, and the Torah as a constitutive document, Israel began to develop into something that can be identified as early Judaism, a religious and ethnic designation.

The prophet Ezekiel is the greatest witness to how the Babylonian exiles understood themselves while in captivity. After the exile we find the prophetic books of Haggai, Zechariah, Malachi, and Joel contributing to this new religious identity. In addition, scholars believe that major portions of the book of Isaiah belong to these historical periods. So-called "Second Isaiah" (Isa 40–55) is usually dated to around 550 BCE, just before the liberation of the exiled Israelites by the Persians. Also, the collection known as "Third Isaiah" (Isa 56–66) is often dated to the early restoration period, possibly centered around the rededication of the temple in 515 BCE. The discussion of Isaiah in this book will cover the whole book, though particular emphasis will be placed on those sections that are undoubtedly from the preexilic period.

Principles of Historical Interpretation

Before turning to the issues of theology and literary features of the prophets, it will help to identify three principles of historical interpretation as related to the prophetic books.

The first thing to do when reading a text from the prophets is to identify the historical context of the passage under consideration. This historical context might be the same as the one generally applicable to the traditional author of the book, though it might be from a later time or different place. For example, the book of Amos is addressed to an Israelite audience around the year 750 BCE. The prophet talks almost exclusively about the coming destruction of the northern kingdom. However, the end of the book contains two oracles that predict the restoration of the southern kingdom. It is reasonable to conclude that a scribe inserted these two oracles as Amos was integrated into the larger prophetic corpus. It is interesting, of course, to read these oracles as the last word to eighth-century Israel, which is how the editors have presented them. It is also important, however, to think about why these later oracles may have been included and what impact they have on the book as a whole.

Second, readers should use their imagination to place themselves in the shoes and in the mind of the prophet. Imagine what the person saying these words would have felt or experienced in the moment of their delivery or composition. Also, imagine what the people hearing or reading these words would have felt or experienced. What was the prophet trying to convince the audience to believe or to do? Why? What was at stake in the decisions facing these people in their time and place?

Third, try to understand these texts as part of a larger ongoing conversation within Israel and Judah. Biblical texts were the arena in which Israel and Judah collectively processed and discussed the things that happened to them across time. Of course there were many places and opportunities for them to talk, debate, and pray. However, the only one that survives for us to study is the Bible, and we should always

Introduction

try to understand it against the backdrop of Israel and Judah's ongoing history and developing culture, religion, and theology.

In the prophetic books we encounter texts that were spoken and written at the time of these momentous events. We also find texts that reflect later prophetic activity that have been incorporated back into the original tradition. Therefore, the final form of a prophetic book is complicated and rich and always in need of careful historical analysis.

Literary Features

This section introduces topics that will be covered in more depth in the chapters to follow. Understanding a prophetic oracle depends very much on understanding the words and phrases actually used in that prophecy. The problem is that most prophecy takes the form of poetry, which is sometimes difficult to understand. Interpreting the literary techniques of the prophets is a tentative, ongoing process, but one that will hopefully provide an enjoyable challenge rather than become a source of frustration.

One area of literary techniques employed by the prophets is that of poetic artistry. The single most difficult thing about reading the prophets is that they are written largely as poetry rather than prose. We are unfortunately not exposed to poetry as much as we should be in our society, and we have forgotten much about how to interpret the various poetic devices we encounter. Of course, we read the prophets in English, so there is at least one level of remove between us and the original poets. Good translations will reproduce the poetic structure and language of the Hebrew original, and this is a case where comparing different translations can be very helpful. We will look at the use of imagery, metaphor, and symbolism as they arise in the prophetic books.

The most common poetic technique in biblical poetry is parallelism, which is when there are two or three lines in a row that state the same basic idea. The value of parallelism is that it enables the prophet to make two or three attempts to convey a challenging message, and to create a richer tapestry of images to convey the point. As modern readers we can use parallelism to help us decipher a confusing phrase or word; by aligning the parallels we can often learn the meaning of a phrase in connection with its poetic mate. Here is an example from Amos 8:4-6:

> Hear this, you who walk all over the needy,
> > and bring to disaster the poor of the land,
> saying, "When will the new moon be finished
> > so that we may sell grain,
> and the sabbath so that we may sell wheat?
> We will make the ephah small and the shekel great,
> > and deceive people with false balances,
> buying the poor for silver
> > and the destitute for a pair of sandals,
> > and selling what is swept up after threshing the wheat."

There are four sets of parallels in this passage, indicated by indentation. "You who walk all over" and the ones who "bring to disaster" are the same people. They are yearning for the end of religious holidays so they can get back to their financial transactions. They are going to "make the ephah small and the shekel great," but it is not immediately clear what that phrase might mean. From the parallel, however, we know that it means "deceive people with false balances." A Bible dictionary would tell us that an ephah is an amount of grain and a shekel is an amount of money. Imagine, therefore, a balance with too small an amount of wheat on one side and too large an amount of money on the other. These merchants are cheating the common people who come out after the Sabbath to prepare their evening meal. The final parallel has three items that are different, but each one points to a particular way that these corrupt businesspeople are abusing the poor; they are taking advantage of the needy and not providing the basic charity that the law requires.

A second area of literary artistry in the prophets is that of rhetorical strategies. The prophets were not simply speaking for their own benefit or giving their prophecies in private.

Introduction

They spoke to particular people in specific times and places, and their words are meant to persuade their audiences that their message is correct.Usually they wanted these people to *do something* in response to that message. Thus, they used rhetorical strategies to get people's attention and to persuade.

The literary techniques just discussed are themselves rhetorical in nature; the prophets delivered interesting and engaging speeches that drew the audience in through the use of engaging language and descriptive imagery. Another element in the prophets' speech was the use of "reversal," the process of drawing the listener in and then switching things around at the last minute. A good example is found in the first two chapters of Amos, in which the prophet begins by announcing God's judgment on all of God's enemies. As Amos works his way around the map, expressing God's anger at Israel's historical enemies, the hearers become interested and excited. The last nation in the list of God's enemies, however, is Israel itself. The reversal works by having the people buy in to the idea that God will punish wicked nations, but then adds the additional bit of information that Israel is chief in that list.

Another interesting rhetorical strategy is the use of "identification," in which the prophet constructs a parable in which the listeners are meant to identify with one of the characters. There is sometimes a reversal here, where the prophet reveals the identifications at the last minute. Examples of this include the Song of the Vineyard in Isaiah 5 and Hosea's marriage to Gomer in Hosea 1–3. Whereas the listeners may want to identify with the disappointed farmer in Isaiah or the wronged husband in Hosea, the prophet identifies them with the destroyed vineyard and the punished harlot.

A third literary technique that can pose difficulty for readers is the creative use of quoted speech. In any given oracle the "speaker" in the passage may be the prophet or God, but it also may be the people in reality or as satirized by the prophet. It may even be some outside party such as a foreign king. Often these various voices engage in a dialogical back-and-forth that may not be clearly indicated by the text. For example, take a close look at Isaiah 10:5-19 and notice who is speaking in each verse. The speech begins with God speaking about the Assyrian king: "Against a godless nation I send him" (v. 6). Then, in vv. 8-11 we have the words of the king himself, boasting about his violent accomplishments. Verse 8 begins with "For he says," but the "he" is ambiguous; is this next section a further addition to God's speech in the first three verses or someone else? Is the "he" the same person as "his heart" in v. 7? It seems that these are the words of the Assyrian king, showing that what is in "his heart" conflicts with God's purposes for his actions. The same confusion occurs in vv. 12 and 13. The prophet speaks of God, saying, "He will punish." Then he reports that "he says: 'By the strength of my hand I have done it.'" The alternation of speakers shows the contrast between God's actions and the Assyrian king's pretensions. The king's speech is followed by the rhetorical question "Shall the axe boast over him who hews with it?" (v. 15a). Thus, the oracle makes a case for dual agency. The Assyrian king makes decisions and takes action, but God ultimately uses the king's decisions and actions for a larger divine purpose. Such a tool of God's justice (the "axe"), however, is not aware of this larger purpose and will itself be destroyed when it is no longer useful.

Of course, these are not the *actual* words of the Assyrian king, as much as they may sound like an Assyrian king's taunt. The prophet "quotes" these imaginary words of Sennacherib for literary and rhetorical purpose. Other quotations have similar literary purpose and effect, including when the prophet sarcastically quotes the people back to themselves and when he chooses to speak in his own voice *about* God and when he presents the words of God in direct quotation.

These are only a few examples of literary artistry in the prophets, but each oracle in this literature reflects literary achievement. There is no one "right" way to interpret these metaphorical and rhetorical elements. When approached with curiosity and openness, there are many exciting ideas and insights waiting to be uncovered by the reader. It is certainly possible to go too far with this type of interpretation, so one should always be careful to attend to what is actually in the

Introduction

text rather than the mind of the interpreter and to let the text as a whole guide and shape its own interpretation. The prophetic texts demand close reading and hold great rewards for interpreters with creativity and imagination.

Theological Traditions

The most important phrase in all of the prophetic literature is the introductory clause "Thus says the Lord." In this way the prophets assure their readers that they speak an authentic word from God and not merely their own thoughts and agenda. We will see later that Jeremiah makes this fact his defense against opposition; he asserts that he would at times rather not speak the harsh judgment oracles that God has given him but that he literally cannot hold them in (Jer 20:7-9). For interpreters of the prophetic literature, however, the situation is more complex. The prophets speak to their time and place and draw upon a variety of ideas, experiences, and traditions that they hold in common with their listeners. In other words we must explore the background and influences behind the ideas found in the prophets and how they each engage their tradition in the process of crafting a prophetic message for their audience. We should not imagine inspiration to be a mechanical process in which God puts a prophet into a trance and bypasses the prophet's mind and identity to deliver a message. The prophets were not like the operator of a telegraph station, automatically passing along other people's words. They were themselves creative geniuses who critically engaged their communities and brought their own personalities, perspectives, and insights to the process. Christian and Jewish readers consider them to have been inspired by God in this process, but such inspiration does not erase their individuality.

In other words the prophets are God's messengers, but the message they deliver is mediated through themselves and bears the stamp of each prophet's unique identity. Prophets speak to particular people, and they use various rhetorical techniques to persuade them. Therefore, we should try to identify what is unique about each prophetic book, how it grows out of and responds to its historical context, and how each prophet uses the religious and theological vocabulary of the day to craft the message. For example, one important difference among the prophets is whether they tend to draw on Mosaic covenantal ideas (Amos and Hosea), Davidic covenantal ideas (Isaiah and Ezekiel), or some combination of the two (Jeremiah). Recognizing the particular theological traditions that underlie a prophetic oracle will help readers understand better what the oracle says and why it was given.

It is important to remember as well that the prophets must present *arguments* for their theological point of view. Sometimes we presume that things in the Bible are there because they reflect what everyone in biblical times believed and accepted to be true. To the contrary biblical texts were written down because their authors were trying to convince people that their ideas should be believed and accepted. In other words what we see in the prophets (and elsewhere in the Bible) is the record of theological arguments that took place at various points in Israel's history. Interpreting a prophecy requires attention to the "hot button" theological issues of the time and how the prophets engage that issue. Many of these issues will surface in the chapters to follow, but three topics are common to all the prophets: covenant, justice, and worship.

Covenant

There are two primary covenantal traditions in the Hebrew Bible, which we refer to generally as the Mosaic and Davidic covenants. First of all, *covenant* is another term for "agreement" or "contract," and like all contracts, covenants have certain involved parties and specific responsibilities for each side. By looking briefly at the origin and character of these two covenants, we will be able to see how they have impacted prophetic literature.

The Mosaic covenant refers to the agreement between God and the Israelites at Mount Sinai. This story is narrated in

INTRODUCTION

Exodus, but the heart of the Mosaic covenant is the book of Deuteronomy, which is Moses's representation of the agreement that had been made (Deuteronomy means "second law"). The book of Deuteronomy shows many of the features of ancient Near Eastern "suzerainty treaties" between two kings. This kind of treaty was made between a greater king and a lesser king, which means that most of the requirements were placed on the lesser king with the greater king providing most of the benefits. The Mosaic covenant, as a suzerainty treaty between God and Israel, declares that the Israelites bind themselves to follow God's Law in gratitude for God's miraculous deliverance of them from Egypt. As long as Israel is careful to keep the Law, God promises to provide blessings of protection, fruitfulness, and long life. If the people persist in disobeying the Law, however, the contract may be broken, which means they would become subject to God's punishment.

The Mosaic covenant, therefore, is a "conditional" covenant that depended on Israel's keeping of its stipulations, most importantly the Ten Commandments. The Deuteronomistic History (the books of Joshua, Judges, Samuel, and Kings) is greatly influenced by this conditional covenant and explains the destruction of Israel and Judah as God's punishment for the people's disobedience. Notice, for example, the explanation of Assyria's destruction of Israel in 2 Kings 17:7: "This occurred because the people of Israel had sinned against the LORD their God, who had brought them up out of the land of Egypt from under the hand of Pharaoh king of Egypt." This Mosaic tradition radiates through the judgment oracles of prophets such as Amos, Hosea, and Jeremiah.

The second major covenantal tradition in the Old Testament is the Davidic covenant, which refers to the agreement made between God and David in 2 Samuel 7:16: "Your house and your kingdom shall be made sure forever before me; your throne shall be established forever." God says that if one of David's royal descendants is disobedient, God will punish him but will never completely remove the Davidic line from the throne. Thus, the Davidic covenant is ultimately "unconditional," meaning the covenant itself can never be broken by either party. This covenant is part of what might be called Judean royal theology, meaning it provides the theological underpinnings of the Judean Davidic monarchy.

The Davidic covenant is the central feature of a tradition known as Zion theology. According to Zion theology, God had chosen three things for eternal divine protection and favor: the house of David, the city of Jerusalem, and the temple in Jerusalem where God chooses to dwell. Because of the unconditional nature of the covenant, Zion theology asserts that the monarchy, Jerusalem, and the temple are ultimately secure. Isaiah draws dramatically upon this tradition in his words of assurance to Ahaz and Hezekiah, both kings in Jerusalem under threat by foreign powers. This also seems to provide the impetus for the words of the "false prophet" Hannaniah in Jeremiah 28. Hannaniah predicts that God is about to restore the monarchy and to redeem Jerusalem from the hands of the Babylonians while Jeremiah (influenced more by the Mosaic covenant at this point) argues that the Babylonian occupation will continue as God's judgment for Judah's disobedience.

These covenantal traditions support the prophets' underlying logic, whether predicting judgment or salvation. By paying attention to covenantal references, such as Jeremiah's quoting of the Ten Commandments or Isaiah's words about Zion, one can understand why the prophet's words may be effective or convincing to his listeners. This also helps us account for conflict with and among the prophets, as they applied these covenantal traditions differently to their situation.

Justice and Righteousness

Central to the Israelite covenantal system is a strong personal and social ethic. Jesus reflects his Jewish tradition when he remarks that the two greatest commandments are to "love the Lord your God" and "love your neighbor as yourself" (Matt 22:37-40), quoting from Deuteronomy and Leviticus. The Law requires Israelites to show mercy to the weak and defenseless (such as aliens, widows, and orphans), to be fair and compassionate toward laborers and slaves, and to value human life

Introduction

and dignity over monetary success. The various aspects of Israel's ethical system are often collected under the phrase "justice and righteousness."

Consider the queen of Sheba's approving words to Solomon in 1 Kings 10:9: "Blessed be the Lord your God, who has delighted in you and set you on the throne of Israel! Because the Lord loved Israel forever, he has made you king to execute justice and righteousness." Psalm 72:2 echoes the same sentiment in a prayer for the king: "May he judge your people with righteousness, and your poor with justice." The king has a special obligation to establish justice and righteousness in the land and is often criticized by the prophets for not fulfilling these responsibilities.

The burden of justice and righteousness does not depend only on the king. Proverbs 21:3 expresses an idea at home in the prophetic tradition: "To do righteousness and justice is more acceptable to the Lord than sacrifice." The people as a whole have a responsibility to live ethically, committed to God's vision of human relationships. Amos pronounces judgment on those "that turn justice to wormwood, and bring righteousness to the ground" (5:7). Isaiah uses these terms in his hopeful vision of Jerusalem's future: "Zion shall be redeemed by justice, and those in her who repent, by righteousness" (1:27). Jeremiah preaches a sermon in the Jerusalem temple in which he outlines these basic requirements: "Act with justice and righteousness, and deliver from the hand of the oppressor anyone who has been robbed. And do no wrong or violence to the alien, the orphan, and the widow, or shed innocent blood in this place" (22:3).

The prophets assume that the people know exactly what God expects of them. Judgment oracles often have a tragic tone because the people have ignored basic instruction and repeated warnings, to their peril. The prophets denounce rulers who abuse their power to the harm of the poor and defenseless, business leaders who cheat and lie to make money, and religious leaders who stand by without protest while such transgressions take place.

Worship

The first two of the Ten Commandments set forth a vision of Israel's worship life grounded in the exclusive worship of Yahweh. The first commandment is that Israel should have no other gods than Yahweh, and the second is that they should use no images in their worship of Yahweh (an idea known as *aniconism*). These two provisions make Israelite religion quite unique; monotheism is very rare in the ancient world while aniconic worship is almost completely unparalleled. Readers should note the difference between the first and second commandments: the first one prohibits worshiping other gods while the second concerns the kinds of things one may do in the worship of Yahweh.

The Bible claims that the Israelites engaged in widespread syncretism, that is, the importing of foreign religious elements into one's worship. The historical books suggest, for example, that there was a great temptation for Ba'al worship in Israel (1 Kgs 18) and use of various kinds of images in the Jerusalem temple (2 Kgs 22–23). Each of these examples relates to one of the commandments: the worship of Ba'al is a violation of the first commandment, and the variety of things found by Josiah in the temple in 2 Kings 22–23 is a violation of the second commandment.

The prophetic literature also addresses the first two commandments together; the prophets say that the people's illegitimate worship of other gods is made even worse by the fact that they are using images ("idols") in the process. You can find examples of this idea in Isaiah 31:7, Jeremiah 10:1-16, and Hosea 11:2, in which Yahweh laments, "The more I called to them, the more they ran from me; they persisted in their worship of the Baals, and in offering incense to idols." The people, therefore, are breaking two distinct commandments by worshiping another deity and by using an image in their worship. This could be interpreted as two facets of the same sacrificial act or as two separate things being addressed at once by the prophet. The prophets seem congruent with the reform movements of Judean kings Hezekiah and Josiah, who both

INTRODUCTION

attempted to purge religion of syncretistic and iconic elements. However, none of the prophets explicitly mentions these reforms, nor do they appear in the historical narratives about them.

Another important element of worship that we should discuss is the practice of sacrifice. The prophets often speak words against the sacrificial cult, though none more than Amos. In Amos 5:21-23 we read this harsh judgment: "I hate, I despise your festivals, and I take no pleasure in your gatherings for worship. Even though you offer me your burnt offerings and your grain offerings, I will not accept them, and the offerings of well-being of your fatted animals I will not look upon." Hosea says that God desires "steadfast love" rather than sacrifices (6:6), and Micah argues that justice, kindness, and humility are better than even exorbitant offerings (6:6-8).

Sometimes Christians read these passages as a wholesale denunciation or rejection of the Israelite sacrificial system. It is important to note, however, that the prophets do not call for the abolition or replacement of Israel's traditional sacrifices. Rather, they merely point out the hypocrisy and sinfulness of those who practice them. People think they can break God's commands for justice and righteousness and then have their offerings accepted by God without penalty. The prophets say, however, that they may as well do nothing for all the good their rituals accomplish.

The challenge for modern readers is to put the prophets' harsh words about sacrificial practices in the context of their overall message to the people. They try to get people's attention by making strong, even offensive statements. These declarations are not, however, objective theological arguments against ritual worship. In this book we will have the opportunity to look at these passages in more depth, but the main thing to remember is that the prophets see Israel's religious practices as integrally connected with its ethical and moral behavior. Another way to say this is that all daily actions should be acts of worship to God, whether in the world of the temple, the marketplace, or the family.

Reading the Words of the Prophets

Reading a prophetic oracle is often difficult, but sometimes it is deceptively easy. When you encounter a passage that does not seem to make any sense, rather than skipping over it, spend time reading it carefully, and try to restate each verse in your own words. Consider each verse in light of others around it, trying to learn who is speaking to whom and what is being said. When you encounter a familiar passage, try to forget what you know and read it again for the first time. By reading slowly and deliberately, one can almost always discover new interpretations and insights.

Reading a prophetic oracle consists of several steps. First, read it quickly for an initial impression. What is the general subject matter? Does it focus on judgment, salvation, or something else? What kinds of images and metaphors are being used and for what purpose? Does it have a beginning, a middle, and an end? What effect does the oracle have on you?

Second, imagine this oracle being delivered in its original context. Who was in the audience, and where were they? What tone of voice did the prophet use, and what facial expressions do you imagine in the crowd? What was the prophet trying to get the people in his audience to do or believe? What effect would the oracle have had on them? In this step it is helpful to read the oracle out loud, with feeling. After you have summarized each verse in your own words, you should be able to vocalize the text clearly and with the proper intonation and emotion. These are texts that were originally spoken, and they were later written down so they could be read aloud by others. This is an occasion when it would be helpful to have more than one translation on hand, as some are more technically accurate and some are more poetically crafted.

Third, think more specifically about the three topics in this section: historical context, theological traditions, and literary techniques. Using the introductions and notes in your study Bible or in a good one-volume commentary, learn something about the historical setting of the oracle. Prophetic books often

INTRODUCTION

begin with a note about when the prophet lived and who the kings were. Also, within the oracles there are historical references to famous people or events. What impact does the historical context have on the interpretation of the oracle? Next, consider the theological ideas found in the passage. Are they connected to ideas in other parts of the Bible? What do they assert about God that is new or different or surprising? Finally, look more carefully at the literary features of the oracle. What kinds of poetic devices do you see, and how do they work in the passage? How does the use of imagery, metaphor, and parallelism affect your interpretation of the passage?

About This Book

By bringing historical, theological, and literary issues into conversation, the goal is to make the prophetic literature accessible and interesting. Each chapter will begin with four sections: an outline of the book, a brief historical overview, an explanation of the important theological traditions addressed by that prophet, and a preview of the most important literary techniques. These sections are not exhaustive. Rather, they are intended to help the reader begin the process of interpretation. Other resources such as study Bibles, commentaries, and Bible dictionaries will be important tools for further reading.

After these opening sections, each chapter will present a survey of that book's major sections, including a closer analysis of representative passages in that prophetic book. The interpretations here are not meant to be exhaustive or authoritative but a starting point for conversation and debate. We will present the "scholarly consensus" whenever one exists but will also make a point to raise controversial arguments where they bring important issues into view.

Reading the prophets is a complex enterprise. It cannot be accomplished quickly or easily, but great rewards come from a sensitive and patient reading of the prophetic literature. Perhaps more than any other kind of literature in the Bible, the prophets lead us to make connections between the historic dealings of God with Israel and our own world. The prophets call their audience to understand the great truths of old in a new light, either by quoting an ancient tradition or alluding to it through poetry or analogy. As modern readers we are drawn to consider how those original listeners would have made these connections in their world and to make connections for ourselves. Sometimes we will encounter these truths in a way similar to those ancient listeners, and sometimes we will hear things quite differently. In any case it is the same voice that engages us, coherent and dynamic.

Note

[1] Donald Gowan, *Theology of the Prophetic Books: The Death and Resurrection of Ancient Israel* (Louisville: Westminster John Knox, 2008) 9–10.

Chapter 1

Amos

Introduction

The book of Amos is the oldest prophetic text in the Hebrew Bible. The narrative backdrop for these oracles seems to be a dramatic scene straight out of a movie: a dusty traveler wanders into town and, speaking with a southern accent, begins to preach. At first he draws the people in with his vivid imagery, commanding presence, and words of judgment against that people's enemies. Once he has his audience in his grasp, however, he begins to name their own sins and failures, denouncing the people as well as their rulers, business leaders, and priests. Finally, the local priest pushes into the circle and commands this strange outsider to go back to the land from which he came. Sneering, the preacher responds with a personal, scathing, and violent prediction of God's judgment on the priest and his family. This unwelcome visitor finally does leave town but on his way out delivers one last judgmental sermon that is shocking and offensive in its dark and violent imagery. He utters the unthinkable, announcing that God is about to destroy not just their nation but every living person within it. With that, Amos wanders vaguely southward, back out of town.

As we saw in the introductory chapter, readers should focus more on the prophetic texts and less on reconstructing the biography and psychology of the prophets. However, it is important to imagine ourselves in the midst of the narrative context as it is structured by the book. The people of Israel in the mid-eighth century BCE were in a state of ease, confident in their security and prosperity. Amos, an outsider from the southern nation of Judah, pierces that naive confidence with a harsh word of judgment. In Amos's prophecies we find many of the basic rhetorical and literary patterns that we will see throughout the prophets, so this book is a great place to begin our exploration.

Historical Context
Israel and Judah

The death of Solomon in 928 BCE led to the unraveling of the political union between north and south that had been forged by his father, David, seventy-five years earlier. The northern kingdom, which kept the name "Israel" while David's line continued to reign in Judah to the south, had always followed a more "charismatic" rather than "dynastic" theory of kingship. In other words they wanted to choose their own king based on his personal qualities rather than simply accept whoever was the "rightful heir." They did not accept the leadership of Solomon's son Rehoboam, so they cast their allegiance on one-time Solomonic official and dissident, Jeroboam (1 Kgs 11:26-40; 12:12-20).

According to the biblical historian, one of Jeroboam's first official acts was to restore the ancient worship practices at the Israelite towns of Bethel and Dan, instituting (again?) the use of a physical image of God, a golden calf, in each place (1 Kgs 12:25-33). This is clearly meant to remind readers of the golden calf made by Aaron at Sinai (Ex 32) and to indicate why God would turn against Jeroboam even after choosing him to rule in place of Rehoboam. It may be that Jeroboam was restoring ancient worship practices that had been suppressed by the unification of worship in David and Solomon's

AMOS

Jerusalem. Even so, ancient Israel was historically a more religiously diverse place than the Bible might indicate.

The central point here is that there was always cultural, religious, and political tension between the northern and southern regions of the united monarchy, and those tensions led to the development of the divided monarchy in the ninth and eighth centuries BCE: Israel in the north and Judah in the south. When Amos travels north to Israel in 755 BCE, the people would not have seen him as "one of us." Judah was a foreign nation, in fact a relatively small and weak neighbor. Israel and Judah shared a language, a history, and a religious tradition, but they were different nations with a different identity and different challenges.

Omri and Jehu

Through most of the divided monarchy, Israel was the more powerful and dominant of the two sister states. Although a single Davidic royal line ruled in Judah, due to its commitment to the "dynastic" model of kingship, Israel enjoyed a series of royal families, coups, and usurpers. The two longest Israelite dynasties were those of Omri and Jehu. Omri began to reign around 880 BCE, and his line included his son, the famous king Ahab, and two grandsons. Omri and Ahab appear in extrabiblical records as formidable kings, and it is Omri who built the Israelite capital city of Samaria.

The usurper Jehu seized the throne in a bloody coup around 845 BCE and established a dynasty that lasted nearly 100 years (2 Kgs 9–10). His grandson, Jeroboam II, reigned forty-one of those years until his death in 746 BCE (2 Kgs 14:23-29). Amos 1:1 indicates that the prophecies of Amos were delivered during the reign of Jeroboam II, and on this basis we can date the book to around 755 BCE. The prophet even denounces Jeroboam by name in Amos 7:10-14. The turbulent final years of Israel will figure in our historical discussion of Hosea and Isaiah, but the time of Jeroboam—and thus Amos—was a period of relative peace, prosperity, and security.

Social and Economic Realities

The Bible has little to say about the reign of Jeroboam II, especially considering the fact that he reigned forty-one years and had political importance in the region. Second Kings notes that he restored Israel's northern and eastern borders, reestablished Israelite control over the Transjordan as far north as the Beqah Valley, and subjugated the Aramean cities of Hamath and Damascus.

More relevant than the exact geographical limits of Israel's control, however, is the fact that the nation during this time was untroubled by foreign military pressure. The Assyrians had not yet begun their westward expansion under Tiglath-Pileser III, and Israel seems to have had control over its own borders and foreign policy. Given Israel's geographical location astride major roadways between Egypt, the Mediterranean, and Mesopotamia, it is reasonable to conclude that economic and political leaders enriched themselves through taxation and other trade duties. This wealth made its way to the official sanctuaries as well, enriching local priests.

Thus, it seems that during the reign of Jeroboam, Israel enjoyed a period of great prosperity. Amos and Hosea both indicate that the economic, political, and religious elite of Israel lived in luxury even though their lavish lifestyle contributed to the further oppression of the poor and weaker members of society. Archaeological evidence supports this view of Israelite society in the mid-eighth century BCE. In and around Samaria researchers have found buildings made with impressive materials and techniques, as well as a collection of commercial receipts on clay potsherds (known as *ostraca*). Fascinating information also comes from a collection of ivory fragments found in Samaria, richly detailed with Egyptian motifs. Amos himself mentions the rich merchants with their "houses of ivory" (3:15), and these objects provide a tantalizing glimpse into the economic prosperity in Israel in the eighth century BCE.

Amos

The Book of Amos

Amos should be dated to about 755 BCE, near enough to the end of Jeroboam's reign to be immediately relevant to his listeners but early enough that the eventual Assyrian invaders would not have been mentioned by name, as they are in Hosea. One reason that Amos's rhetoric is so extreme is that the people are not in a position to hear his message. Given their prosperity and ease, why would they listen to this prophet of doom and gloom? Surely, they would have thought, their blessings indicated God's pleasure and provision! Those who are "at ease in Samaria" and lounging like "cows of Bashan" did not see any major catastrophe on the horizon, so they were dismissive of Amos's word of judgment.

However, starting in 745 BCE, the Assyrian king Tiglath-Pileser III began a westward campaign that eventually overwhelmed Israel and dozens of other local peoples. The destruction of Israel in 722 BCE explains why Amos and Hosea have survived in the Bible; later Judean prophets found in their words a powerful prediction not only of Israel's downfall but a word of caution (and hope) for Judah as well.

Indeed, although the majority of the oracles should be dated to around 755 BCE, the last two oracles in the book come from a later Judean context (Amos 9:11-15). The prophecies of Amos became a literary production created by and addressed to a later Judean community in exile. Thus, the words of a Judean prophet to an Israelite audience finally made their way home into the Judean prophetic canon. For more discussion of these later oracles, see the commentary below.

Theological Traditions

Many important theological ideas are found throughout the prophets, and we cannot be exhaustive in this section. Rather, we will identify a few theological ideas that each prophet seems to have known and engaged, beginning here with Amos. We will also see how theological ideas in later prophets augment and differ from those of the earlier ones. Taken as a whole, the prophetic literature records a breathtaking conversation in Israel and Judah about ultimate questions of meaning in the midst of crisis and change.

Covenant

The fundamental theological category in the prophetic literature is that of "covenant," or the idea that God has entered into some kind of an agreement with the people. One might even argue that "covenant" is the central idea of the whole Bible, and we will consider how the prophetic notion of covenant influenced the New Testament in our last chapter. The word *covenant* includes several different ideas and assumptions, however, and it will be important to identify the aspects of the covenantal tradition from which each prophet draws.

Amos seems to have known the basic tradition of the Sinai wilderness wanderings and been familiar with the Mosaic covenant that emerges from that story. Amos recalls how God brought the Israelites out of Egypt, through the wilderness, and into the promised land (2:10) and made an agreement with them (3:3). Most of the offenses that Amos points out also resonate with the Deuteronomic law. For example, he chastises the Judeans "because they have rejected the law of the LORD, and have not kept his statutes" (2:4), which reflects the language of Deuteronomy about the "statutes and ordinances" that God establishes in the Mosaic Torah. Also, he claims that Israel has lain down beside every altar "on garments taken in pledge" (2:8), which violates the law of Deuteronomy 24:12 that one should not sleep on a garment taken in pledge from a poor person, since it may be their only means of warmth. Many other passages in Amos resonate with Mosaic law in this way.

Worship

It is in the text of Amos that we find the earliest list of the three main Israelite sacrificial traditions that are detailed in

Leviticus 1–4 (Amos 5:22). This list, however, comes in the midst of a wholesale denunciation of Israel's ritual life ("I hate, I despise your festivals," 5:21) and Amos's claim that God had not asked for sacrificial offerings during the wilderness wanderings (5:25). Thus, although Amos seems familiar with the Israelite ritual system, he expresses God's displeasure and even rejection of their worship practices. This harsh criticism does not mean that God prefers non-ritualistic worship or that Amos, as a prophet, is opposed to the priestly world. God rejects Israel's sacrifices and festivals because they have been corrupted by social injustice and have failed to honor the true spirit of the Law. In addition to the sexual and economic sins reflected in 2:6-8, Amos says that the Israelites "transgress" whenever they come to the place of worship because they have oppressed the poor (4:1-5). He says that they dishonor the Sabbath by anxiously waiting for it to end so they can get back to cheating their customers (8:4-6). For Amos, worship practices only have integrity and efficacy when they are part of the larger fabric of justice and righteousness.

Judgment and Hope

The most common unit of prophetic speech is the "judgment oracle," and Amos's judgment speeches are famous for their imagination and power. But what is the rhetorical purpose of such judgment oracles? Sometimes "oracles against the nations" may function as *salvation oracles* for the listeners. Judgment oracles against the listeners themselves may serve as a warning and provide a step toward salvation if the people listen and reform (e.g., Jonah's preaching in Nineveh, although this salvation did not make Jonah very happy).

At other times, judgment oracles are simply announcements of God's coming wrath. In Amos we come the closest to judgment oracles that imply little or no hope for the future. Judgment oracles seem to mirror the language of a courtroom sentence in which the defendant is pronounced guilty and given his or her just punishment. God says in Amos 8:2 that "the end has come upon my people Israel; I will never again pass them by," which indicates that the covenant of old has been broken and that Israel is no longer God's people. The result of this catastrophe is total destruction of Israel. After a series of gruesome descriptions of divine punishment in chapter 8, God says in 9:1b that "those who are left I will kill with the sword; not one of them shall flee away, not one of them shall escape."

Is this judgment and destruction truly universal? Is Amos completely without hope? The last two oracles (9:11-12, 13-15) provide a hopeful vision of restoration, though as we shall see, these have been added by a later Judean prophet. Prior to these two short oracles, Amos seems to announce a complete judgment of God on Israel without reprieve or hope for forgiveness.

Literary Features

Judgment Speeches

We have already discussed the literary form of the "judgment speech" in the Introduction chapter, and such is the basic genre used in every chapter of Amos. The key to this genre is to look for the point of inflection in which the prophet shifts from the indictment ("because you have done these things") to the announcement of judgment ("therefore, thus shall be the punishment"). How the prophet modifies and augments this basic form is one key to his literary and rhetorical mastery. For example, the extended oracle in chapter 5 shifts to indictment in vv. 11 and 16 (notice the use of "therefore"), which highlights the addition of vv. 14-15, an unusual passage in the book that offers the possibility of hope and restoration. These verses do not seem to fit the theology of the book in general or the form of the present oracle. Noticing the form of the judgment oracle in this case helps us think about the theological and literary complexities in the final form of the book.

Amos

Oracles Against the Nations

Amos begins with a series of "oracles against the nations," a genre of prophetic speech that we find in most of the other prophets (e.g., Isa 13–21; Jer 46–51; Ezek 25–32; Nahum). The basic theological assumption in these oracles is that the God of Israel and Judah is in fact the sovereign Lord of all the world, and that this God controls global events to fulfill the larger divine purposes. Israel and Judah are often the weaker victims of the nations receiving God's judgment, so these oracles function as hopeful words of comfort to God's people.

Amos uses this prophetic form in a different way, however. He begins his speech with a series of oracles against Israel's neighbors and bitter enemies. His purpose is not to comfort his listeners but to show that God is in the process of bringing all wicked people to justice. As it turns out, Israel is the last member of that list of nations who will receive God's judgment. For more discussion of Amos's use of an oracle against the nations, see the exegetical discussion below.

Rhetorical Questions

In the Introduction chapter we suggested that interpreters should read the words of the prophets aloud with dramatic expression. The tone of voice and attitude behind the words makes a world of difference to their interpretation and meaning. The most common tone of voice in Amos seems to be bitter sarcasm, occasionally rising to sharp fury. Amos has none of the emotional connection with the people evinced by Jeremiah (e.g., Jer 9:1) or the humble questioning we see in Habakkuk (Hab 1:2-4). He is angry and dismissive, disgusted by all that he knows of Israel's social, economic, and religious abominations.

One vehicle for the prophet's sarcasm is his use of rhetorical questions. These rhetorical questions imply their own answer and point out what should be obvious. The prophet uses these "obvious" observations to show how Israel has failed to acknowledge basic truths, corrupted as they are by their sin and wickedness (see Amos 3:3-8 ["Do two walk together unless they have made an appointment?" v. 3]; 6:12a ["Do horses run on rocks? Does one plow the sea with oxen?"]; and 9:7a ["Are you not like the Ethiopians to me, O people of Israel?" says the LORD].

Rhetorical Quotations

The prophet also quotes his audience's point of view back to them in order to illustrate the ridiculousness of their situation. Of course, it is unlikely that anyone ever *said* these words or would have said them. However, the prophet insists that their actions speak louder than words and that they will recognize themselves in these quotations if only they would be honest with themselves. Consider the following examples.

2:12	"You . . . commanded the prophets, saying, 'You shall not prophesy.'"
4:1	"Hear this word, you cows of Bashan . . . who say to their husbands, 'Bring me something to drink!'"
6:13	"You who rejoice in Lo-debar, who say, 'Have we not by our own strength taken Karnaim for ourselves?'"

8:5	"[Hear this, you who say], 'When will the new moon be over so that we may sell grain; and the sabbath, so that we may offer wheat for sale?'"
9:10	"All the sinners of my people shall die by the sword, who say, 'Evil shall not overtake or meet us.'"

In each of these, the use of rhetorical quotation makes the oracle more vivid and powerful, hopefully piercing the shield of self-righteousness constructed by his audience.

Vision Reports

Amos presents a series of vision reports of increasing intensity, each beginning with the refrain "This is what the Lord God showed me" (7:1, 4, 7; 8:1). Each of these visions is of a natural or physical phenomenon that evokes the image of divine judgment: locusts, fire, a collapsing wall, and a deceptively rotten basket of fruit. Rhetorically, these vision reports are vivid and memorable, but they also establish the prophet's authority as one who has access to God's words and intentions. Finally, they demonstrate God's increasing impatience with Israel's sins. During the first two visions, the prophet is able to intercede on behalf of the people, but by the fourth vision God has decided to destroy the nation, and there is nothing the prophet or anyone can do about it.

Biographical Narrative

Many of the prophets include a section of biographical narrative, sometimes written from the perspective of the prophet himself and other times from a later, third-person point of view. Amos 7:10-17 interrupts his series of vision reports with a brief report of a conflict between Amos and the high priest of Bethel, Amaziah. Embedded within this third-person narrative is a fascinating account of Amos's prophetic call. He says, "I am no prophet, nor a prophet's son; but I am a herdsman, and a dresser of sycamore trees, and the LORD took me from following the flock, and the LORD said to me, 'Go, prophesy to my people Israel'" (7:14-15). This story validates the prophet's authority as one called by God to deliver a divine message. Contrary to Amaziah's contention, he is not a political dissident or interloper with his own agenda, but simply a divine messenger. Such "call narratives" are present in Isaiah 6, Jeremiah 1, and Ezekiel 1–3 and resonate as well with the story of Moses (Ex 3) and Samuel (1 Sam 3).

Commentary

Amos 1–2

1:1-2

Amos begins with the customary historical dating formula, which indicates when and where the prophet was active. As we saw earlier, these dating formulas help interpreters place the words in their historical context, although we must take care to remember that some portion of the book was added by later editors. Even so, we can read the book in its final form as an address to this implied audience as well as to real audiences later in the stream of tradition.

The introduction also states that these words were "two years before the earthquake." Historians cannot say exactly when this earthquake occurred, so it is not helpful for dating the book. Even without knowing the date of this disaster, the reference establishes a rather ominous tone for the book from the beginning. Amos's descriptions of judgment often draw upon imagery of natural disasters, including an earthquake-type event in 9:1, and this enigmatic little note subtly sets the tone for the ensuing oracles.

1:3–2:5

If we imagine these oracles as the first words Amos speaks to his gathered crowd in Bethel, they seem to be well chosen. Here, the prophet offers God's judgment on Israel's enemies, one by one. He works his way around the map, jumping from Aram in the northeast, Gaza in the southwest, the Phoenician city-states in the north, and Edom, Ammon, and Moab in the southeast. At each of these stops on the compass, the prophet insists that God will visit judgment upon their enemies, and the audience agrees.

Each of these prophecies is structured with a counting formula: "for three transgressions of X, and for four, I will not revoke the punishment." This type of rhetorical device is found as well in the Psalms and Wisdom literature and lends a powerful and memorable structure to the prophet's opening oracles. What ties this series of oracles together, beyond their common structure, is that each of them describes a situation of violence and dehumanization. The Arameans ("Damascus") have plundered Gilead like a farmer reaping grain in a field, while Gaza, Tyre, and Edom are denounced for supporting slavery and the deportation of entire communities. The Ammonites also are singled out for plundering Gilead, but in their case they have "ripped open pregnant women . . . to enlarge their territory" (1:13). In each of these cases, Israel's enemies have committed serious human rights violations in the pursuit of their own economic or political interests.

Amos finishes with Israel's immediate neighbor to the south: Judah. It may be that this last stop on the tour caused a sharp intake of breath or two, but despite their shared history, Judah and Israel had been at odds for many of the years of the divided monarchy. The oracle against Judah in 2:4-5 is rather more generic, indicating only that Judah has rejected the Law of God and been corrupted by lies just like their ancestors. It may be that this is a later addition to the book, and it certainly sounds like the standard denunciations of Judah by the Deuteronomistic historians who wrote during the exile. Such a later dating is not essential, however, since it matches well the oracles that follow it.

2:6-16

The last of Amos's "oracles against the nations" is the climactic moment in this first part of the book, for here the listener discovers that the last and perhaps worst of God's enemies is Israel itself. God's gaze has toured around the map, skirting the borders of Israel, but finally rests in judgment on a people who should know better. They have broken the covenant with God in multiple, fatal ways.

Israel is condemned for two specific violations in this opening section: economic injustice and religious apostasy. Verse 6 says that wealthy Israelites "sell the righteous for silver and the needy for a pair of sandals." This seems to describe a form of debt slavery in which poor people are driven into servitude because they cannot afford to pay small debts (the cost of "a pair of sandals," for instance). As mentioned earlier, in v. 8 there is a reference to lying at night "on garments taken in pledge." This is a direct violation of Deuteronomy 24:12, which says that garments taken from poor people as collateral for a debt must be returned to their owner each evening since those garments might be their only source of warmth at night.

Notice as well what these people are doing with these mistreated collateral items: they are lying on them in the sanctuary *while engaging in vile religious sexual practices.* Verse 7 says that fathers and sons are having relations with the same woman in the sanctuary so that God's name is profaned. This refers to a common practice in the ancient world known as "sacred prostitution," or *hieros gamos* ("sacred marriage"). In this ritual, sexual activity would be used to ensure fertility, an enactment of the union between a god and the earth or the blessings bestowed by a fertility goddess. Such practices are naturally forbidden in every phase of Israelite religion, and the prophet seems revolted by the very idea.

The religious apostasy of these decadent Israelites extends as well to the silencing of their religious leaders, the normal source of teaching and correction that might have stood against these violations of the covenant. Verses 11-12 say that God had raised up prophets and other highly committed leaders like the Nazirites, who are devoted to religious purity and service (Num 6), but the people have defiled and disempowered them.

The sins that Amos identifies in Israel seem rather tame compared with the violence and rape perpetrated by the other nations in chapters 1–2. However, Israel is held to a higher standard because it had been God's special possession, whom God had rescued from their enemies and brought out of Egypt (vv. 9-10). Because they have rejected God's vision for their communal and religious life, that protection will not cease, and Israel will find itself attacked (vv. 13-16). Amos returns to this theme consistently, especially in 3:1-8.

It is likely that outside invaders will be the danger from whom the people are unsuccessfully trying to flee, but the prophet attributes this destruction to none other than God. This image of the people trying to run away from God's wrath in futility will appear throughout the book, most shockingly in chapter 9.

Amos 3–6

In this central unit of the book, Amos announces God's coming wrath on Israel through a series of judgment oracles. He focuses on the sudden and inexorable quality of God's punishment that will fall of them, and these images sparkle against the backdrop of a people living in security, ease, and prosperity. Their very wealth has become their downfall as it leads to a series of economic and social injustices as well as a corrupted confidence in their goodness and God's continued blessing.

Amos 3–4

Amos begins by building the case that God's anger and punishment of Israel are justified (3:1-8). Why should Israel be destroyed utterly when their sins seem much less severe than the ones listed in the first two chapters? Because they are the only nation to have a special and covenantal relationship with God. As he often does, Amos evokes a common image, two people who are joined in a common bond ("Do two walk together unless they have made an appointment?"), and then subtly twists that image into a shocking and horrifying thought. God and Israel, he says, are not only like two people with an appointment; they are like a lion and its prey, like a bird and its trap, like a trumpet and the disaster it announces. This first section is cast as a series of rhetorical questions, which has the effect of making the events described in them perfectly normal and unsurprising. A lion doesn't roar when it has no prey, and a bird doesn't get trapped when there is no trap! Likewise, if a city is destroyed, of course it is God who has caused it to happen. If a prophet speaks judgment, of course that means God has given that prophet the message of doom. Israel, receiving such a message, should not feel that something unexpected is happening to them. The coming punishment of Israel is a simple matter of cause and effect, and Israel should be able to apprehend their situation clearly.

In Amos 3:11 the prophet rules out the possibility that a faithful remnant might be saved from the coming invasion when "an adversary shall surround the land, and strip you of your defense." Might it be that certain people are more guilty than others. Perhaps the ruling class only? In his characteristically sarcastic way, the prophet says that, yes, they may expect some part of their community to survive the coming catastrophe, as a piece of an ear is rescued from a lion. Their "remnant" will be body parts and charred fragments of house furniture. Consider also the vision of total destruction in Amos 6:9-10, in which there are only enough people left alive to bury the dead.

If such a punishment seems too harsh for the circumstances, remember the rhetorical context of Amos's oracle. The people are at ease and secure, seeing themselves as blessed by God and in no danger. As the prophet points out in 5:18-20, the moment of greatest danger is often when people think that danger has passed and that they are now safe. In order to get his message across to such an audience, the prophet must speak loudly and harshly, using extreme rhetoric to get their attention and make his arguments. Moreover, the very nature of the people's sin makes them impervious to the prophet's message. Their wealth has insulated them from the realities of everyday life. They live in lavishly decorated summer and winter homes (3:15), and even their wives are lazy and drunk oppressors of the weak and poor (4:1). The "cows of Bashan," along with the rest of their families, are about to be ripped, literally, from their comfortable, stupefying homes and carried into foreign exile (4:2-3).

When that moment comes, especially if they do not heed the words of Amos, they will be surprised and dismayed because they consider themselves to be proper and righteous. They are faithful to their worship duties in the regional sanctuaries, offering their proper sacrifices and tithes. He says that their worship in local altars such as Bethel and Gilgal is worthless because they have neglected the true ethical and religious responsibilities that support and give meaning to ritual worship. It did not have to be this way, Amos laments, or come to this final destruction. As the prophet lays out in 4:6-13, God has already executed a series of warning actions, including famine, drought, blight, plague, and widespread death. Even these terrible calamities have not reminded the Israelites of their dependence upon and reverence owed to God.

Amos ends with a doxology of praise for "the Lord . . . of Hosts," literally, "Yahweh of the Heavenly Armies" (4:13). This was most likely one of the oldest "epithets" (i.e., descriptive phrases) for God and emphasizes God's creative power and the majesty of the divine warrior. Such a description is difficult for modern readers to accept uncritically, but it is consistent with Amos's extreme rhetoric. In other prophetic books, the description of God as "Lord of Hosts" is used to give the people comfort in the face of foreign enemies. God has the power, the prophets declare, to protect the people from harm. Amos says that this same power can be used for punishment as well. For more on the question of "the Old Testament

God," see the section on the New Testament in the final chapter.

Amos 5–6

Amos 5 includes the most familiar passage in the book: "But let justice roll down like waters, and righteousness like an ever-flowing stream" (5:24). This verse has been important to social justice preaching in the modern world. It was quoted most famously by Martin Luther King Jr. in his "I Have a Dream Speech" and in the "Letter from Birmingham Jail," in which he calls Amos "an extremist for justice" and links him with figures such as Paul, Jesus, Martin Luther, Abraham Lincoln, and Thomas Jefferson. Given what we have already seen from Amos, however, it is clear that these waters are not the cleansing, pure waters of a waterfall or shower; they are a flooding torrent, washing away all people and property in their destructive path. Verse 6 compares God's justice to a raging fire burning up the house of Joseph (i.e., Israel). Whether by water or fire, the result is the same. In a similar vein chapter 5 begins with a funeral lament for "virgin Israel," who has been killed in the field, cut down in her youth, full of wasted potential.

These chapters contain specific details of the sins that have led to this bleak state of affairs (5:10-12; 6:1-6). The Israelites have subverted justice by corrupting the judicial system. They have used their power to take further advantage of the weak rather than protecting them from harm. They have constructed their business practices in order to get the most money possible with the least possible investment, often with bribes and other dishonest means. They have lived in luxury while poor people suffered around them, drinking wine and moisturizing their skin while the nation crashes into ruin. These rich and indolent fools will be the first to suffer when the destruction comes (6:7). They will be punished for turning "justice into poison" and "the fruit of righteousness into wormwood" (6:12), which resonates with God's lament in Isaiah that justice has become bloodshed and righteousness has been replaced by the cry of the persecuted (Isa 5:7). Amos 8:4-6 contains a similar description of Israel's deceitful business practices and disdain for true worship.

In Amos 5:18-20 we also find an important early reference to the common prophetic motif "the day of the Lord." As we shall see in other prophetic books, especially Zephaniah, the "day of the Lord" is "that day" in which God will come as judge, warrior, and king to set the world right. In most cases this day is a positive event for God's people, the day of their salvation from foreign enemies. Amos implies that the Israelites expected such a day, but what they have not realized is that they are among the list of God's enemies to be judged! The day of the Lord is "darkness," not "light," he insists, because it will result in punishment, not salvation, for Israel. He develops two particularly vivid images to describe their situation: they are like one who gets away from a lion and relaxes for a second, only to be attacked by a bear, and like one who comes into the safe haven of home, only to be bitten by a snake in the thatching of the wall (5:19). In other words the moment when Israel feels the most secure is actually the moment of their greatest danger.

Amos 7–9

Amos 7–8

The central feature of Amos 7–8 is a series of vision reports, each following a set literary structure: God "shows" something to Amos; God asks Amos what he "sees"; Amos responds with a description of the vision; finally, God interprets the meaning of the vision in light of Israel's coming judgment. In the first two cases Amos successfully intercedes on behalf of Israel, but finally the weight of Israel's sin is too much, and God announces the complete rejection and total destruction of Israel (8:1-3).

Three of the visions are natural and related to agriculture: locusts, wildfire, and a rotten basket of fruit. These images evoke the idea that a naturally good thing (in this case, the land) has been destroyed and perverted, as Israel has rotted away in its sin. The third vision in the sequence is of a wall that has fallen out of plumb and will be destroyed, which communicates the same idea but outside of the agricultural context (the image of a rotten wall collapsing in judgment is found as well in Isa 30:13 and Ezek 13:10-12).

The final vision (the "basket of summer fruit" in 8:1-3) is notable for two reasons. First, its interpretation turns on a pun found in the original text: "summer fruit" and "end" sound almost identical in Hebrew. Also, Amos says that "the end has come upon my people Israel," which might be rephrased as "my people Israel are no more" or "Israel is no longer my people." This expresses the unequivocal annulment of the covenant between God and the people, a fact driven home by Amos's allusion to the exodus and the Passover, when he says "I will never again pass them by." The covenant that God made with Israel at Sinai after the exodus is no longer in effect, and they cannot expect such a gracious act of deliverance again in their future. Understood in their covenantal context, these verses are among the most bleak and horrifying in the Bible.

Embedded within these four visions is a fascinating brief biographical "prophetic report" of a conflict between Amos and Amaziah, the local priest in Bethel (Amos 7:10-17). Amaziah has accused Amos of treasonous speech against King Jeroboam II and has sent a letter (unanswered?) to Jeroboam on the matter. Amaziah confronts Amos in the square and tells him to return to Judah: "Earn your bread there, and prophesy there" (v. 12). The implication of Amaziah's demand is that Amos is a member of the professional class of prophets and can choose to travel to where the prophesying is easiest and most profitable.

Amos responds by denying that he is such a professional prophet, saying, "I am no prophet, nor a prophet's son" (7:14). He does not mean that his biological father wasn't a prophet, but rather that he is not a member of the guild of prophets, apprenticed into the profession as Elisha was apprenticed to Elijah (see 1 Kgs 19; 2 Kgs 2). Amos asserts that God had called him from his actual profession, "a herdsman, and a dresser of sycamore trees" (v. 14), probably a middle-upper-class business owner, and sent him to *this place* with *this message*. How could he not deliver that message, and on what basis could Amaziah refuse to let it be heard? Amos then delivers to Amaziah a brutal prediction that the priest will die in exile as his children are killed and his wife prostituted. It is important to remember that Amaziah is not receiving a special or extra-severe punishment. Such things are going to befall everyone, and there is nothing that Amaziah or anyone can do about it.

Amos 8–9

After the final vision report in 8:1-3, the remainder of chapter 8 presents a judgment landscape that foreshadows the apocalyptic imagination of later prophets and of some modern novels and movies, such as Cormac McCarthy's *The Road*. Amos describes a catastrophic earthquake (8:8) and the darkening of the sun during the middle of the day (8:9). Such images of natural disasters show up in all of the prophets, but they gain their fullest expression in texts such as Ezekiel 32:7, Joel 2:10, Mark 13:24, and Revelation 6:12, hallmark texts in the developing apocalyptic tradition.

Amos says that the people living through such times will experience great suffering from famine, thirst, disease, and mourning. Their suffering will be not only physical, however. They will have "not a famine of bread, or a thirst for water, but of hearing the words of the Lord" (v. 11b). It is a common prophetic motif that part of God's punishment will be the cessation of prophecy and other forms of access to God's truth and will. Passages such as Isaiah 28:11-13, Ezekiel 14:9, and 1 Kings 22:20 suggest that God might actively distort the prophetic message in order to confuse and debase the sinful people. This text and others like it emphasize that the presence and availability of an authentic word from God is a gift and a treasure; when it is gone or squandered, people experience something much worse than physical loss or pain.

The vision in Amos 9 takes this bleak view of the future further, even to an incomprehensible point. Earlier we saw that Amos's view of the future is negative and absolute; there will be no last-minute salvation and no righteous "remnant" to be saved for future restoration. Amos drives this point home by developing the most startling example of "reversal" in the book, the rhetorical technique by which something familiar and good is turned around to become an image of horror and judgment.

Amos says that God plans to cause a catastrophe, seen here as the crumbling of the sanctuary upon the heads of its worshipers (9:1), but then to chase down and kill whoever may survive this initial strike. He makes this scene even more powerful by placing the words in God's own speech: "Those who are left I will kill with the sword; not one of them shall flee away, not one of them shall escape" (v. 1b).

From here, the prophet creates a twisted reversal of Psalm 139, the famous affirmation of God's universal and enduring presence in times of trouble. The psalmist prays, "Where can I go from your spirit? . . . If I ascend to heaven, you are there; if I make my bed in Sheol, you are there" (139:7-8) and goes on to say that God can find the needy one even way across the ocean, and there "your right hand shall hold me fast" (139:9-10). Amos reverses this image to say that God will pursue and kill the guilty ones even if they dig into Sheol, climb up to heaven, hide on the mountain or at the bottom of the sea (Amos 9:2–3). (Sheol in both of these texts is used as a directional term, the lowest that one can dig into the earth as opposed to climbing up into the sky.) The central pivot of this oracle is at the end of v. 4: "I will fix my eyes on them for harm and not for good."

So the psalmist and Amos both assert that God has knowledge of every movement of each person and the power and reach needed to find them at any place in the wide creation. Amos turns this around to point out the perhaps obvious but overlooked fact that God's knowledge, power, and reach might be used in service to divine wrath as well as divine love.

In no way can we affirm these words of Amos to be uplifting, edifying Scripture. It would be difficult to read Amos 9:1-4 in a worship service and end with the traditional "the Word of the Lord; thanks be to God!" However, Amos's oracles are rooted in his time and place, and if we interpret them in light of the situation he faced, they are easier to absorb, if not celebrate. Also, these oracles are one part of the larger prophetic literature that includes this perspective while also going much further in integrating God's justice with God's larger plan to redeem the world from its brokenness.

That larger prophetic context is evident in the last two oracles of the book, Amos 9:11-12, 13-15. As we suggested in the "Theological Traditions" section, there is good reason to suppose that Amos 9:11-15 originates from a later time and place. These two brief oracles predict that God will repair "the booth of David that is fallen," restore the city, and bring a renewed era of peace and prosperity. The cities will be rebuilt, the population restored, and the agriculture will be so bountiful that the reapers will not have time to finish their job before it becomes time again for sowing (9:13).

Notice that these are the most optimistic prophecies in the book, indeed the only ones that predict any kind of positive outcome in the future. Notice as well that the restoration that will take place is not actually for Israel, the northern kingdom, but for Judah (i.e., "the booth of David," 9:11), and that from the perspective of the oracles, the booth of David is currently lying in ruins, its people scattered in exile, "plucked up out of the land" (9:15). Therefore, we can conclude that the thoroughly pessimistic judgment oracles of Amos made their way southward to the survivors of Judah's own catastrophic destruction at the hands of the Babylonians in 586 BCE. From the perspective of these prophetic "tradents" (i.e., scribes who curated and edited the prophetic literature during and after the exile), Amos was clearly correct about the fate of Israel, and his message explained as well the righteous judgment of God against Judah 150 years later.

Unlike Amos, however, these later prophetic voices were not pessimistic; they had hope that God would restore the fortunes of Jacob and establish a blessed future in which the people could live again in harmony with God. They added these last two oracles in order to integrate the message of Amos into the fuller prophetic tradition that includes both the reality of judgment and the hope of salvation.

Chapter 2

Hosea

Introduction

The book of Hosea is the second of two prophetic books that originated in the northern kingdom of Israel. Whereas Amos spoke during the reign of Jeroboam II to a community that was prosperous and secure, Hosea's oracles follow the death of Jeroboam in 743 and address the much more tumultuous environment leading up to the destruction of Israel in 722 BCE. His prophetic book shares much of Amos's judgmental rhetoric and is even more rhetorically vivid. However, Hosea draws specifically on the traditions of Exodus to address the question of *why* God is sending this judgment on Israel. Due in part to his covenantal framework, Hosea goes beyond Amos to suggest that the coming punishment is not the end of the story, that Israel might "turn" from its sins and that God might "turn" from judgment to mercy.

The text of Hosea is difficult in many places, and its literary structure is fragmented and repetitive. If one reads the book straight through, there is not much of a literary arc between the narrative sections of chapters 1–3 and the final promise of restoration in chapter 14. On the other hand, this whole section has a coherence that comes from its sustained attention to 1) God's prior provision for Israel, 2) Israel's thoughtless rejection of God, and 3) God's inevitable punishment of the rebellious people. This basic sequence occurs in a circular fashion in the book, each time drawing on different metaphors to express the situation. In the pages to follow, we will examine Hosea's theological program as well as his groundbreaking metaphorical language that became central to later prophetic rhetoric.

Historical Context

The superscription to the book says that Hosea prophesied during the reign of Jeroboam II (who died in 746 BCE), but the southern editor has included several later kings of Judah (Uzziah through Hezekiah) who reigned through the end of the century. Hosea presumes a situation in which Israel is already under pressure from the Assyrians, but it ends most likely before the fall of Samaria in 722 BCE. There have been attempts to connect specific verses in the book to particular historical events, but such efforts are necessarily tentative. Of more value is to know the general historical outline of Israel's final two decades and how those events are reflected in the perspective and tone of the book (2 Kgs 15–18).

Jeroboam II's son Zechariah reigned only six months before he was assassinated in public by the conspirator Shallum. The chaos unleashed by Shallum came back upon him, as he was killed after only one month by Menahem, a brutal usurper who reigned ten years in part because of his (expensive) allegiance to Assyrian king Tiglath-Pileser III. Menahem's son Pekahiah reigned two years before he was assassinated by Pekah, the captain of his guard turned conspirator and usurper. Second Kings 15:27 says that Pekah reigned twenty years, but this must be a textual error since he reigned only during the two- to three-year period leading up to the destruction of Damascus by the Assyrians in 732 BCE (see the discussion of Isa 7–8). Pekah had allied himself with Aram against Assyria, and Israel's penalty for this disloyalty was to see most of its territory annexed by Assyria directly. The city of Samaria alone remained independent where Pekah ruled, followed by his assassin, Hoshea, who reigned for the final nine years.

The historical events leading up to the destruction of Samaria in 722 BCE are unclear, but what we do know is that Tiglath-Pileser III had been succeeded in 727 BCE by his son Shalmaneser V. During that transition of power, Hoshea must have sensed an opportunity and decided to withhold tribute from the Assyrians, hoping for Egyptian assistance (2 Kgs 17:4). Shalmaneser captured Hoshea and laid siege to Samaria itself. After three years Samaria fell to the Assyrians in 722 BCE. During this time the Assyrian kingship had passed to Sargon II, and he instituted a severe resettlement program in which tens of thousands of Israelites were exiled to other parts of the Assyrian Empire. Israel ceased to exist as an independent nation, and no political entity by that name existed until the establishment of the modern state of Israel.

A few passages in Hosea seem to mention these historical events. In Hosea 8:4 the prophet says that "they made kings, but not through me." The plural use of "kings" here may simply be a general statement on Israel's larger history, or it may be a reference to the six kings who reigned in the nine years after Jeroboam II. As we see in Isaiah 2 and 29–30, the prophets are skeptical of Israel (and Judah's) efforts to save themselves by appealing to Egypt and other foreign help. Hosea 7:11-12 says, "Ephraim has become like a dove, silly and without sense; they call upon Egypt, they go to Assyria." As we discussed, Menahem had paid tribute to Assyria (2 Kgs 15:19-20), a fact noted as well in an Assyrian tablet known as the Iran Stele. Hosea says that like a "silly" bird fluttering this way and that, Israel only delays the inevitable with its unstable foreign policy. It is possible that Hosea 10:3 is a reference to the final, chaotic months of Samaria's existence. After Hoshea was imprisoned by the Assyrians, there was technically no king reigning in Samaria for up to three years. Hosea quotes the people as saying, "We have no king, for we do not fear the LORD, and a king—what could he do for us?" Again, this could be a literal reference to that specific time period or a general critique of how lightly the Israelite people regarded authority, whether human or divine. He describes this thinking as "mere words," whose result can only be destruction and exile to Assyria (10:6).

The first edition of Hosea probably appeared in Israel before the fall of Samaria in 722 BCE, but the final form is a Judean production. In chapter 1 the text contrasts the punishment of Israel ("not pitied" and "not my people") with the mercy that God will show Judah (1:7) and suggests that Judah will possess the land that has been vacated by the exiled Israelites (1:11). Hosea 11:12 says that Israel is filled with lies and deceit while Judah "still walks with God" and "is faithful to the Holy One." It would make sense that these small references would have been added by later Judeans who used Hosea to explain the downfall of Israel while still holding out hope for Judah to survive the Assyrian threat. Critical words, however, are also spoken against Judah as the sin and judgment of Israel and Judah are jointly addressed in three places (6:4; 8:14; 12:2). These pronouncements are likely original to the prophet.

Theological Traditions

Many theological terms used in Hosea also figure prominently in other prophetic books. We have already discussed the ideas of covenant, justice, and worship in some detail, and each of these is central to Hosea as well. In the context of God's prior election and blessing of Israel, the people are expected to fulfill certain ethical and religious obligations to God and also to each other. Hosea masterfully connects these three ideas in the extended allegory of his marriage to the prostitute Gomer (1–3). God's covenant with Israel, the prophet says, is comparable to the mutual obligations of a marriage agreement. Israel, however, has acted like an adulterous wife in its worship of Baal and veneration of idols and so must be punished. The faithlessness of Israel has actually annulled the covenant, which is reflected in the names of Hosea's children, "Not-my-people" and "Not-pitied" (1:6-8). Hosea holds out hope, however, that God will be merciful, forgive Israel's sins, and rehabilitate their relationship (2:14-23).

The central problem that Hosea identifies in Israel brings up a new theological concept: the knowledge of God. The problem with the adulterous wife, for example, is that she "did not know" that God was the source of her blessings (2:8). After this first part of the book, there are many references to Israel's lack of knowledge of God (4:1, 6; 5:4; 11:3) that leads directly to their destruction. Hosea 4:6, for instance, says that "my people are destroyed for lack of knowledge," which is caused by the fact that their religious leadership has "rejected knowledge." The priestly and prophetic leaders of Israel have a responsibility to know God and to teach the truth to the people, but they have failed in their duty. Thus, the people fall into all kinds of immorality and false worship (4:7-19), from which the priests even gain some satisfaction (4:8). When the husband (= God) restores her (= Israel), she will "know the LORD" (2:20).

Hosea evokes several other key theological terms, including *hesed*, translated in the NRSV as "steadfast love." This is a key covenantal term for God's unilateral and unconditional commitment to Israel within the Davidic tradition. In Hosea, however, it is used rather to describe the wholeness and integrity of human relationships. It is the term used to characterize the rehabilitated "marriage" between God and Israel in 2:19. In Hosea 10:12 *hesed* is the fruit of the field that is sowed with righteousness, and in 6:6 God declares that such "steadfast love" is what God desires, along with "knowledge," as opposed to sacrifices and burnt offerings. It seems that the knowledge of God, expressed through a genuine spirit of steadfast love, will result in a healthy and blessed community.

Finally, the prophet uses the word *shub*, or "return," in several significant ways. This term describes the turning away from God that has happened in Israel. They turn toward empty things (7:16), so God will repay their sins with judgment (4:9; 12:2, 14), and Israel will even find itself returned to Egypt, the reversal of their salvation from Egypt during the exodus (8:13; 9:3; 11:5). *Shub* also describes the possible, but for now unlikely, turning of Israel back to God (3:5; 5:4; 6:1; 7:10). In addition, the term *shub* can also be applied to God. In the future God may turn back toward them in mercy after the divine anger has turned away (14:4). God will "return" the blessings of the people (6:11) and never return to the former days of punishment (11:9, "again" in the NRSV). Even if the people are exiled, they have the hope of "returning" to their homes and living in safety (14:7). As is clear from the above discussion, the term *shub* is flexible and ambiguous and can be used in different ways (as can the English terms "turn" and "return"). The prophet uses this word repeatedly to set up the basic situation of Israel. Their only hope lies in turning back toward God in repentance and hoping that God will turn to them in mercy and no longer in wrath.

Literary Features

The first three chapters of Hosea constitute a "prophetic report" of Hosea's tragic marriage to the prostitute Gomer. It is sometimes referred to as "prophetic autobiography," but notice that the first chapter is in third person while the second chapter consists primarily of the words of God, thinly pictured as a wronged husband, talking about faithless Israel. Chapter 3 then returns to first-person narrative and might be considered autobiography, although all of chapters 1–3 are biographical, broadly speaking. It is possible that the account in chapter 3 was the initial version of the story and was later enhanced with more details and theological reflection. Hosea 3 resembles the prophetic reports in Isaiah 7–8, in which Isaiah incorporates three children and two of their mothers into the delivery of his oracles against Israel and Aram.

The comparison between God and a jealous husband, and between Israel and his faithless wife, is a metaphor. Metaphors are perhaps the most important tool in the prophetic toolbox, but Hosea employs them with immense creativity. He describes Israel's sins against God as "whoredom," especially their use of images/idols in worship and their "chasing after" Baal, even after chapter 3. In Hosea 4, the people "play the whore" by engaging in practices of divination (4:12; i.e., the use of ritual to tell the future), by making sacrifices in unapproved locations associated with fertility cults (4:13), and by engaging the services of temple prostitutes (4:14; a practice also associated with fertility rituals). In Hosea 9:1 the prophet makes the metaphor more specific; instead of a general promiscuous sexuality, Israel is compared to professional prostitutes who get paid to have sex in public places: "You have loved a prostitute's pay on all threshing floors." In other words, they have done these practices not only for their own pleasure but also in their efforts to please their foreign masters (8:9).

Hosea also describes Israel as "a stubborn heifer" that won't be led in the right direction (4:16; 10:11) and "like a heated oven" (7:4) that scarcely needs any preparation at all to pursue wickedness. They are like a "silly dove" that flies back and forth between foreign masters (7:11) and a "wild ass wandering alone" when those hopes for foreign salvation turn to nothing (8:9).

Also notable are the variety of metaphors for God. In addition to the central metaphor of God as a wronged husband, Hosea draws upon a range of natural imagery to describe God's judgment and mercy. Hosea describes God as being "like maggots to Ephraim, and like rottenness to the house of Judah" (5:12) and like a "lion" that will "carry off, and no one shall rescue" (5:14; cf. 11:10). God's wrath will be "like water" (5:10), similar to the rolling down of the judgment waters in Amos 5:24 (cf. Isa 8:7 and 28:17). God had encountered them first as young grapes (9:10) and a healthy young palm (9:13), but their fruit was wicked (10:1-2), so God will chop down their pillars.

Blind to the depth of their trouble, Israel hopes that God will appear "like the showers, like the spring rains that water the earth" (6:3), which is an unrealistic expectation. However, the end of the book holds out the hope that God may be "like dew" and like a tree with lovely fragrance and shade, allowing Israel to flourish like a healthy grape vine in a pleasant garden (14:4-7).

Metaphorical language always has an "is/is not" quality. The purpose of the metaphor is to make a specific claim about the thing being described. God is *like* a jealous husband in one or two specific ways. However, to say so is to acknowledge as well that God *is not* like a jealous husband in many ways. The proper interpretation of biblical metaphor carefully identifies what the prophet is saying without extending the comparison beyond its limits. Of course, even with this caveat these metaphors can still be theologically limited or troubling. Is it right to compare God to a jealous husband who publicly humiliates his wife or kills her children (Hos 2:2-4)? Many interpreters today choose to read "against" the text in these cases, resisting the metaphor and rejecting its implications about God. Whether we accept this metaphor as applicable and true, reject it as immoral, or something in between, the conversation must be careful and sensitive to those who have suffered under abusive conditions.

Commentary

Hosea 1–3

This passage contains the story of the prophet Hosea's marriage to the prostitute Gomer. God tells Hosea to take a "wife of prostitution" or a "woman of whoredom." This second noun might mean *prostitution* or *fornication*, but in general the book does not distinguish between professional and casual modes of sexual promiscuity. In fact, there is not much information in the story about Gomer's identity nor about the true nature of their relationship. Whatever the details, she is faithless to her husband and pursues sexual gratification with a number of partners. Hosea compares the character of this type of woman to Israel, a nation that owes God its fidelity and gratitude but chooses to worship other gods through idolatry. The text presents the story of Hosea and Gomer in the third person and in an outline form that sits rather transparently over the theological purpose of the story. Rather than concerning ourselves with the biographical details, in the final analysis we should read the story of Gomer primarily as an extended allegory for the relationship between God and Israel.

Gomer bears three children to Hosea: a boy named Jezreel, a girl named Lo-ruhamah, and another boy named Lo-ammi. The names of these children communicate the prophet's message in much the same way as the three "sign children" of Isaiah 7–8. "Jezreel" refers to the bloody coup that brought Jehu into power, which is narrated in 2 Kings 9–10. Jehu kills Jezebel and all of the remaining household, friends, and priests of King Ahab in the valley of Jezreel (2 Kgs 10:11). Hosea's prophecy might be dated near the end of the reign of Jeroboam, the second to last king in the line of Jehu.

The final two names foreshadow the end of Israel's covenantal relationship with God. The term for "pity" in the name Lo-ruhamah, or "not pitied," is used in a special way for God's mercy in Exodus 33:19 and in the central affirmation of the covenant found in Exodus 34:6: "The LORD [is] a God merciful [*rahum*] and gracious, slow to anger, and abounding in steadfast love and faithfulness." Likewise, God's promise in Exodus 6:7 that "I will take you as my people, and I will be your God" lies behind the name of Hosea's third child, Lo-ammi, or "not my people." The names of these children indicate that Israel, previously God's own covenantal people and recipients of God's mercy, will no longer be "God's people." Echoing the weighty proclamation of Amos 8:3 that "the end has come upon my people," the naming of these children predicts the end of God's covenant with Israel.

The significance of the story of Gomer and her children goes well beyond their names, of course. The very circumstances of their birth provide an explanation for why Israel will be judged. Hosea 2:2 addresses the children, asking them to "plead with your mother, plead—for she is not my wife, and I am not her husband." The relationship between God and Israel is envisioned as a fragile marriage between a husband and his rebellious wife. Chapters 2 and 3 focus more specifically on the story of Gomer and the parallels between her and Israel. Some aspects of this story make more sense in the context of ancient marriage than they do in our day. Most notably, there is a profound power gap between the husband and his subservient wife, which explains the unilateral demands he makes upon the woman and his violent punishment of her transgressions. Such domination is no longer acceptable today, even in traditional marriages, and so the metaphor may be problematic for modern readers.

When the husband chooses his wife, he "takes" her from the house of her father and is now responsible for her and for her behavior. Consider the brief recasting of the story in Hosea 3:1-5. Verse 2 says that the prophet "bought her for fifteen shekels of silver and a homer of barley and a measure of wine." Therefore, it would be misleading to compare this marriage to modern notions of love and courtship. The relationship seems one-sided from the beginning, which continues when the husband outlines the rules of their marriage in v. 3: she shall not have sexual relations with any other man, "nor I with you." The first part is normal, but abstinence even between them reveals that this marriage is more an experiment or demonstration than a real union between two people in love.

This seemingly odd marriage makes more sense if we focus on its theological interpretation: the connection between God and Israel, in which such a power gap and one-sided command structure is more appropriate. The prophet suggests that God has chosen Israel unilaterally, due to no merit of its own. God has provided everything that Israel needs to flourish: food, security, and blessing (2:8-9). Astonishingly, rather than being grateful for God's election and provision, Israel has squandered its blessings by lavishing them upon other gods (2:8, 13).

God's response to Israel's short-sighted unfaithfulness is to punish the nation publicly and severely. Nearly every preexilic prophet expresses this idea, but Hosea's use of the marriage metaphor makes this text powerful and shocking. Hosea says of Gomer, "I will strip her naked and expose her" (2:3), and "I will uncover her shame in the sight of her lovers, and no one shall rescue her out of my hand" (2:10). Interleaved with these two statements are several references to deforestation that apply more to the land of Israel than to a wife: "I will . . . turn her into a parched land" (2:3), and "I will lay waste her vines and her fig trees" (2:12). As an angry husband might seize the fine clothes and jewelry of a faithless wife, so God will parch and devastate the land that provides Israel with the food and drink used in idol worship. Finally, Hosea says he will "allure her, and bring her into the wilderness, and speak tenderly to her" (2:14), paving the way to a renewed relationship and physical restoration. The scene in v. 14 may not be as "tender" as the NRSV translation implies, especially considering that "the wilderness" is not normally the place where a husband woos his wife. Rather, the idea here is that the woman has been abased and ashamed, isolated from all comforts and community, and now returns to her husband because she has no other options.

As a description of God's punishment, instruction, and eventual redemption of Israel, this text is at home in the prophets and in the mainstream of biblical theology. As a description of a husband-wife relationship, it is offensive and troubling. The violence and public shaming of Gomer is too close for some modern readers to the experience of abusive husbands and abused wives. The sentiment that he can do whatever he wants and that no one will be able to step in to rescue her from his hands is a haunting reminder of the tragic prisons of marriage in which many women find themselves. The violence described here is slight compared to other passages in the prophets, most notably Ezekiel 16 and 23. Readers must engage these texts in sensitive and complex ways, trying to understand the prophetic rhetoric in its own context while recognizing that our contemporary situation must temper how we understand and express God's judgment and wrath.

Hosea 4–8

The middle chapters of Hosea loosely take the form of a "covenant lawsuit" against Israel. The term *rib* is translated "indictment" in the NRSV, replacing the less specific King James Version rendering of "controversy." The judgment oracles beginning in chapter 4 present a cascade of evidence against Israel, proving that the nation has broken the covenant and failed in their obligations. The "judgment oracle" form follows the legal pattern of indictment and punishment, but the reference to a *rib* here makes that connection explicit. A person found guilty under the law on the basis of objective evidence has no place to complain about unjust treatment. So Israel should not be surprised or chagrined about the punishment they receive. Those who might object to the situation—Israel's priests and prophets—are ordered to refrain from accusations against God, "for with you is my contention" (4:4). The justice of God is unassailable, which God is prepared to demonstrate.

As discussed in the section on theological traditions, Israel's fundamental problem in Hosea is a lack of the "knowledge of God." This idea appears in 4:1 ("There is no faithfulness or loyalty, and no knowledge of God in the land"), in 4:6 ("My people are destroyed for lack of knowledge"), and in several other passages. Israel's religious leadership is supposed to provide knowledge of God, but they have failed in their duty, committing even conspiracy and murder (6:7-10). As a result of this corruption and dereliction of duty, the people of Israel turn to divining rods for information (4:12), break the basic commandments of the Law (4:2), engage in sexually immoral religious rites (4:12-13), sacrifice to idols (8:4-5), and are generally dissolute and lewd (4:18; 5:7; 7:4). The situation is tragic, but there is so much collective guilt that neither the prophet nor God feels the kind of empathy that we see in Jeremiah or Habakkuk.

The priests are guilty—"the more they increased, the more they sinned against me" (4:7)—but so are the people, and all will fall in judgment together: "and it shall be like people, like priest" (4:9). Part of the tragedy of the situation is that the people sometimes try to worship God and to commit themselves to act righteously. According to the prophet, however, their efforts are self-seeking, hypocritical, and ineffective, and it would be better if they did not even try. In 4:15 the prophet says, "Do not enter into Gilgal, or go up to Beth-aven, and do not swear 'As the LORD lives,'" an echo of Amos's denunciation of worship at Gilgal and Bethel (Amos 5:5). Hosea later says that the sacrificial worship at Gilgal is where "every evil of theirs began" (9:15; 12:11). Their sacrificial practices will now have no benefit for them because even though they seek the Lord, "they will not find him; he has withdrawn from them" (5:6).

God goes so far as to predict that the coming judgment will motivate Israel to acknowledge their guilt and ask for mercy. In a scathingly sarcastic oracle God predicts what they will say and how fast their repentance will fail (5:15–6:6). Recognizing the price that they have paid for their lack of knowledge of God, they will say, "Let us know, let us press on to know the Lord" (6:3). However, God knows that their feelings will fade quickly, evaporating like the morning dew (6:4). God desires steadfast love (*hesed*) and knowledge of God rather than their sacrifices or empty emotional cries (6:6). Whenever God moves to forgive and heal Israel, at that very moment their falseness and wickedness is revealed, and "their deeds surround them" (7:1-2).

Indeed, every effort that Israel makes to address their current situation is corrupt and counterproductive. They "multiply altars" so they can make sacrifices for their sin, but these altars have become—ironically—"altars for sinning" (8:11). Feeling vulnerable in the midst of a world in crisis, they have chosen kings and princes to protect them. They do this, however, without God's knowledge, and so they go to their own destruction (8:4). They have built palaces and fortresses in which to hide, but God's fire will "devour his strongholds" (compare the repeated use of this phrase in Amos 1-2). Finally, Israel has tried to defend itself by making political alliances with both Egypt and Assyria, but now among the nations they will become "a useless vessel" (8:8). The prophet sums up these efforts at self-preservation in a famous line: "For they sow the wind, and they shall reap the whirlwind" (8:7a). In many ways, both politically and religiously, Israel has created the conditions of its own destruction. Every move they have made away from God, and even toward God, will turn back upon them in God's judgment.

Finally, notice the variety of rich metaphors used in these chapters. We saw the extended allegory of Israel as a faithless wife in chapters 1–3, and such language appears in this section as well (4:10-13; 5:3). Moreover, Israel is compared to a "stubborn heifer" (4:16), a silly dove caught in a trap (7:11), a "wild ass wandering alone" (8:9), and "a heated oven, whose baker does not need to stir the fire" (7:4). Israel cannot be convinced to follow the correct path, resisting all truth in stubbornness, but when it comes to doing iniquity, they are always ready and willing. Of course, this fire of iniquity that burns inside them eventually devours them. Hosea 7:5-7 states that the officials become heated up with wine, which leads to anger that eventually erupts in violent insurrection, with the result that "all their kings have fallen." Considering the tumultuous history of the Israelite monarchy after Jeroboam, Hosea's description of palace intrigue seems quite accurate. When it comes to their dealings with foreigners, Israel is like "a cake not turned" (7:8); they think their plans are moving along well, but in reality they are being burnt up underneath where no one can see. Only the prophet can reveal the true desperation of Israel's plight.

Hosea 9–14

The final chapters of Hosea continue the previous section's somewhat repetitive images of judgment and punishment. The general movement in this section is from Israel's wickedness to God's punishment and, finally in chapter 14, to God's eventual restoration of Israel. Along the way there are individual units that make important contributions to the overall message of the book.

Chapter 9 of Hosea begins with the familiar charge of harlotry, in this case specifying the professional form of sexual debauchery: "You have loved a prostitute's pay on all threshing floors" (9:1). This mention of the threshing floor begins a remarkable series of verses held together by a leaping progression of related images. Evidently it was common for prostitutes to visit the threshing floor during the harvest time, when men slept amid their work. Hosea connects the image of the threshing floor with that of the wine vat, which was used as well during a harvest, and then predicts that the grain and wine will fail them (9:2). If there is no grain or wine, they will not have materials to use in their idolatrous rituals (9:4). Indeed, all of their festivals will cease, and their finer luxuries will be stolen by foreign enemies (9:5-6). Looking closely, we see how the prophet moves in steps from the image of harlotry to that of Israel being plundered by the Egyptians and Assyrians. If we read these verses too quickly, they may seem random or scattered, but in fact there is an inner logic and order to the passage. Such is true of many passages in the prophetic literature.

Hosea is not immune to the criticisms faced by other prophets such as Amos and Jeremiah. Hosea denounces prophets who fail to do their duty (4:5), but in 9:7-9 he defends the prophets who speak the truth during a bad situation. Others may say that "the prophet is a fool," but they should remember that the prophet is merely "a sentinel," the messenger of God's activities, not the one responsible for the vision he reports. The term for "sentinel" here is the same used in Habakkuk's resolve to serve as a "watchman" for God's coming justice. The term is used in 2 Samuel 18:24-27 for a person standing on the wall and reporting down to the king what he sees in the field outside the city. In Ezekiel 33:6 it is clear that the sentinel of a city is responsible for warning the people when he sees danger coming and will be held responsible if he does not do so. Thus, the people should listen to the prophet/sentinel and not be angry if they do not like what he reports.

The descriptions of Israel's sin and God's punishment are diverse and arresting. In 9:10-14 God says that Israel became God's people when they were young and budding "like the first fruit on a fig tree" but that they went on to become corrupt and detestable. Therefore, God shall punish them by eliminating their fertility and sending infant mortality (9:11-12). When the prophet asks God to "give them a miscarrying womb and dry breasts" or when God says "I will kill the cherished offspring of their womb" (9:16), the text evokes horrifying images of divine violence that hit very close to home for anyone who has struggled with infertility or lost a child. This prophetic rhetoric of violence is harsh and difficult, and readers have the freedom to resist such images or read against the prophet. However, it does help to understand these violent images within the larger rhetorical canvas of the prophet. In this case, this harsh imagery is connected specifically to the previous image of early Israel as fertile and budding.

Chapters 10–11 employ a variety of agricultural and natural images to reflect on the arrogance of Israel in turning away from the God who has empowered, protected, and blessed them. Verse 10:1 says that Israel is like a "luxuriant vine," a prosperous nation but one that has used its wealth to pay for corrupt ritual practices. God established them in their land, but they have turned their back on God and declared arrogantly, "We do not fear the LORD" (10:3). Before, they were like "a trained heifer," an animal prized for its beauty and never required to work, but now they must plow and labor (10:11). They might have sown righteousness and reaped *hesed*, but instead the prophet tells them that they have "plowed wickedness" and "reaped injustice" (10:13). In their arrogance, they turn away from God, thinking that their power is enough to sustain and protect them. They did not recall how much their power and safety depend on God's continued protection.

In one of the more emotionally affecting passages of the book, God casts himself as the father of a wayward child, Israel (11:1-11). As a father, God raises his child with love and tenderness, training and protecting him, feeding and healing him. However, the son decides to run away amid foreigners and idolatrous practices. God responds to this rebellion with the cry of a wounded parent: "How can I give you up, Ephraim? How can I hand you over, O Israel?" (11:8). In this moment of compassion, God chooses to have mercy on the wayward child. At this point the metaphor shifts and pictures God as a lion and Israel as his wandering cubs. A powerful and awful figure, God roars like a lion, and "when he roars, his children shall come trembling from the west" (11:10). They come at his call because they know that in that powerful voice is their protection and salvation in a dangerous world. They tremble, however, at the majestic power of their father.

The final section of the book, chapters 12–14, takes a wider view of Israel's history and considers what the future might hold. The prophet refers to various incidents in the history of Jacob (12:2-4; 12:12–13:1) and in the history of Israel in the wilderness (13:4-6). This is a story of election, blessing, and protection of Israel during vulnerable times, but Israel responds to God's blessings with indifference and rejection. Verse 13:6 says, "When I fed them, they were satisfied; they were satisfied, and their heart was proud; therefore they forgot me." God now faces a difficult decision: whether to punish Israel utterly or to relent from punishment. Chapter 13 ends with a bleak and brutal answer to that question: God decides to punish without compassion, not to "ransom them from the power of Sheol" or to "redeem them from Death" (13:14). Echoing the horrific language of Amos 1:13, God says that their children will be dashed into pieces and their pregnant women ripped open (13:16).

If the book had ended with such a horrible vision (and some people have argued that it originally did), it would agree with the pessimistic outlook of Amos. It may be that the last chapter of hopeful prophecy was added by a later hand, in the same way as the last two oracles of Amos. However, there is more theological complexity and possible hope for restoration throughout the book of Hosea, and so this final chapter can certainly be read as an integral part of the original text. It begins with the command, "Return, O Israel, to the LORD your God" (14:1), a common thread throughout the book. The positive images in this final chapter resonate with earlier motifs and passages in the book. The people offer God the "fruit of the lips," as opposed to the "fruit of lies" (10:13). They will no longer depend on Assyria's help (5:13) or make idols out of normal objects (13:2). Instead of being like maggots and rottenness (5:12), God will be like the dew. Most notably, the book ends with the affirmation that righteous behavior grows out of true knowledge of God (14:9). In this harsh and difficult prophetic book, Hosea attempts to convey a saving knowledge of God that may help the people avoid the total destruction that they justly deserve.

Chapter 3

Isaiah

Introduction

The book of Isaiah is the longest of the prophets and undoubtedly the most complex and difficult text to introduce in a brief survey. The book that bears the name of the prophet "Isaiah" actually is the product of three or more different prophetic voices spread over 200 years. Scholars have long recognized that different historical situations and prophetic voices are represented in the book, but determining exactly which texts date from which period and how they came together is a challenging process. We may never know which parts of the book may be attributed to the historical figure of Isaiah, the Jerusalem prophet from the second half of the eighth century BCE. Certainly there is a division at the beginning of chapter 40, but even the section known as First Isaiah (chs. 1–39) is the result of later compilation. Whatever its internal history, the final form of Isaiah is an object of great beauty and significance.

A professor once said that you could write an entire "theology of the Old Testament" using only the book of Isaiah. That is an exaggeration, but not much of one. The book contains formative material from before, during, and after the exile. It deals with the political and religious issues that face a people living with, or without, a king. From a historical, theological, and literary point of view, Isaiah is a magisterial achievement that encompasses the range of Israel's story, faith, identity, and hope.

Historical Context

In some ways, the context of Isaiah involves the whole "Historical Context" section in the Introduction. It might be helpful for readers to review this section before diving in to Isaiah itself, as well as to read 2 Kings 15–25, 2 Chronicles 36, and Ezra.

First Isaiah

Much of the first section of Isaiah (chs. 1–39) derives from the prophet Isaiah himself, who lived in Jerusalem during the last half of the eighth century BCE. According to Isaiah 6:1 the prophet was called "in the year that King Uzziah died," or roughly 742 BCE. Scholars do not agree on the exact dating for the Judean kings of the eighth century BCE or whether Isaiah 6 is a "call narrative" rather than just an event that happened during his ministry. In any case Isaiah's ministry extended from 742 through the end of the century. Three crucial events happened during this time period. First, Judah was invaded by an army of Israelites and Arameans in 734 BCE while Ahaz was on the throne. Their goal was to replace Ahaz as king and force Judah to join their regional coalition against the encroaching Assyrians. This event stands behind the "sign children" prophecies of Isaiah 7–8.

Second, the Assyrian advance continued undeterred (the Aramean capital Damascus fell in 732 BCE) and eventually led to the destruction of Israel and the fall of Samaria in 722 BCE. This was the end of the northern kingdom of Israel. Many refugees from Israel fled southward, probably bringing with them key texts that became part of the biblical tradition, including Amos and Hosea. Judah survived the Assyrian occupation because of Ahaz's cooperation and payment of tribute (2 Kgs 16:7-8). It continued as an Assyrian vassal until it was defeated by the Babylonians near the end of the seventh century BCE. (For more on that sequence of events, see the discussions of Nahum and Habakkuk.)

The third major event took place during the reign of Ahaz's son Hezekiah, who reigned from 725 (or 715) until about 697 (or 687) BCE. The biblical history celebrates Hezekiah as a great religious reformer and a strong king, and archaeological evidence seems to confirm that his reign was active and prosperous. Hezekiah took steps that enabled him to rebel against the Assyrians, including the construction of a water tunnel in Jerusalem and the establishment of central repositories for grain, wine, and other commodities. He withheld tribute from the Assyrian king Sennacherib, which prompted his invasion of Judah in 701 BCE, an event that echoed in significance for over a century (2 Kgs 18–19; Isa 36). Sennacherib quelled the rebellion but was not able to overrun Jerusalem or remove Hezekiah as king. Second Kings attributes this to the nighttime attack on the Assyrian army by an angel of the Lord (2 Kgs 19:35-36). This seemed to many, Isaiah included, to be confirmation of God's special protection of Jerusalem, as expressed in Zion theology.

Second Isaiah

The second major phase of prophetic activity in the book of Isaiah begins in chapter 40 and dates to the final years of Judah's exile in Babylon, probably around 550 BCE. The tone, style, and theological emphasis of this middle section of Isaiah is strikingly different from what came before. The prophet of "Second Isaiah" (chs. 40–55) comforts the people (40:1) and assures them that God has begun the process of forgiving and restoring them.

Whereas the first thirty-nine chapters of Isaiah are filled with specific historical references and proper names, there is only one proper name after chapter 39, that of the Persian leader Cyrus (Isa 44:28; 45:1). Cyrus led a Persian revolt against the Medes in 550 BCE and eventually assumed control of the crumbling Babylonian Empire in 538 BCE, founding the

Persian Empire. The oracles in Isaiah 40–55 mention Cyrus but describe him in the process of consolidating his rule rather than having already taken over the Babylonian territory. Thus, we might date these oracles to the time just after 550 BCE and situate them among the Judeans living in captivity in Babylon.

The theological interpretation of Isaiah 40–55 centers around the experience of "diaspora" Israel, the "scattering" of the Jewish people that began in earnest with the Babylonian exile. Instead of finding judgment oracles addressed to a royal house in power in Jerusalem, these passages reflect on Israel's hope of salvation and on the nature of God, who has the power and inclination to gather and restore the people to their land.

Third Isaiah

Finally, many scholars see a third division in the book (chs. 56–66), dating to the time of the early postexilic period, perhaps just before and after the rebuilding of the temple in 520–515 BCE. It is possible that this final section also originated in Babylon with chapters 40–55, but several specific references to temple worship situate the prophecies in early postexilic Jerusalem. Isaiah 63:18-19, 64:10-11, and 65:18-19 imply that the temple has already been destroyed, as it was in 586 by Nebuchadnezzar. Isaiah 56:6-8 suggests that some of the Israelites have already returned from exile and that temple worship has been restored.

When the Persians took over the former Babylonian territories, Cyrus decreed that people who had been displaced by the Babylonian policy of resettlement could return to their ancestral lands. Ezra 1 casts the "edict of Cyrus" as God's specific provision for Israel. An object known as the "Cyrus cylinder" contains the text of a decree similar to that in Ezra 1, though it does not mention the Israelites. The Persians turned Judah into a province (Yehud) and installed a governor over them (Sheshbazzar and later Zerubbabel, who is pictured as the messiah in Hag 2:20-23). The Persians gave money and support to the Judeans for rebuilding the temple and reconstituting their religious hierarchy and laws. The "Torah" took its

Isaiah

final form during this period, with the approval of the Persian authorities.

Theological Tradition

The book of Isaiah is complex and theologically rich, and we can only begin to scratch the surface of this multilayered text. The theological perspective of the book shifts as its historical context changes. The book initially focuses on judgment, emphasizes God's mercy and power in the middle, and ends by articulating a vision of blessed life together in a redeemed community. The time between the earliest and latest texts in the book may be as long as 250 years, and many different factors influenced its development.

Even so, the book shows a remarkable degree of theological coherence given its long history. The sixth-century BCE prophets who incorporated new materials were guided by the original tradition and probably saw themselves as extending the theology of Isaiah to new generations. We will look at individual sections in the commentary, but here let us survey a few theological ideas that tie the book together.

First, Isaiah is the most important source for "Zion theology," the form of Judean royal theology that emphasizes the importance of 1) Jerusalem as God's chosen city, 2) the temple as the place where God's presence dwells, and 3) the Davidic royal line that God established forever. Zion theology is intricately tied to the tradition of the Davidic covenant found in texts such as 2 Samuel 7 and Psalms 89 and 132. These texts promise that God will never abandon the royal line; even if individual kings are punished, God's original promise to David will stand forever. This theology encourages confidence, hope, and pride among citizens and rulers of Jerusalem and underlies Isaiah's advice to "stand firm" in the face of foreign invasion (Isa 7). In the later sections of the book, especially Third Isaiah, Jerusalem/Zion is the center of God's universal plan of salvation.

A second theological emphasis in the book is that God is the Lord of history who manipulates international events to fulfill divine purposes. In its earliest history, the people of Israel considered God to be their patron deity, whether the personal god of Abraham, the "divine warrior" of the tribes, or the powerful king enthroned in the temple in Jerusalem. The prophets take this idea in a new direction, however, suggesting that God did not only rule over Israel (in protective and punitive ways) but that God could also "rouse up" foreign nations to do God's will. In Isaiah (and Habakkuk to come) the idea of God as Lord of history includes the notion of "dual agency," in which God may use a person as an agent while that person is still accountable for their own decisions. This dual agency appears through the Assyrian king who destroys nations as part of God's judgment but who is himself punished for his arrogant boasting (Isa 10:5-19), and also through Cyrus, the Persian leader whom God empowers to liberate Judah from the Babylonians. In fact, Second Isaiah refers to Cyrus as God's "anointed," or, in Hebrew, "messiah" (45:1). God's use of royal figures to establish justice and righteousness appears as well in the "messianic" prophecies of chapters 9 and 11.

Second Isaiah takes the idea of God as Lord of history a step further, emphasizing that God is the creator of the world and indeed the only true divine being in the universe. In passages such as 44:6, 45:22, and 48:12-13, God declares that "besides me there is no God" and "I am God, and there is no other." These passages are the natural extension of previous theological ideas such as God's lordship over history and Israel's exclusive worship of God (*henotheism*), but they are the first places where we see unambiguous monotheistic affirmations.

Isaiah is also emphatic about what kind of God this is, besides whom there is no other. God's character is embodied in the requirements of justice and righteousness on one side and through God's mercy and desire to save on the other. Isaiah resonates with Amos's and Hosea's calls for economic and social justice and for the exclusive worship of God alone. Also like those earlier prophets, Isaiah emphasizes that Israel's ritual life is worthless if it is not rooted in practices of justice, care for the poor, and support for the vulnerable. Against

Amos's pessimistic outlook, however, Isaiah affirms that God cannot simply forget Israel and Judah. With the slightest contrition and humility, Israel may see God's forgiveness and mercy.

If we connect the ideas of monotheism and God's commitment to justice and mercy, it is easy to see why Isaiah goes even further to say that God has a plan for redemption that encompasses not only Israel but the whole world. It is an *inclusive* vision rather than a *pluralistic* one, meaning that although Israel is the center from which God works, other nations may participate in and benefit from God's work in Jerusalem. This outward-looking perspective is one of the most enduring contributions of Isaiah to biblical theology.

Literary Features

Terminology

One important element in understanding Isaiah's prophecy is recognizing to whom the prophecy is addressed and, if possible, where it fits within Isaiah's long timeline. During the early phase of Isaiah's ministry, he addresses both the northern kingdom of Israel as well as his native Judah. After Israel is destroyed in 722 BCE, Isaiah speaks about the desolation of the north and the continued threats to Judah. During and after the exile, the term "Israel" came to refer mainly to the remaining bearers of Israelite identity, the Judeans. Therefore, in early passages Israel (and related terms such as Samaria, Ephraim, and Jacob) refers to the northern kingdom while Judah refers to the southern kingdom. After the destruction of Jerusalem in 586 BCE, Israel has broader application to the people as a whole, centered now in Jerusalem of Judah, the Persian province of Yehud.

Call Narrative

Isaiah 6 contains the "call narrative" of Isaiah, similar in theme to that found in Amos 7 and Jeremiah 1 but literarily closer to the call of Moses in Exodus 3–6. Both Moses and

Isaiah experience a "theophany," or direct appearance of God, as they are commissioned for a specific prophetic role. For more on "theophany," see the discussion in Habakkuk, but notice here that Isaiah's vision of God is an awe-inspiring scene accompanied by thunder, smoke, and earthquake. Like Moses, Isaiah initially protests that he is not worthy of the vision he receives, expressing regret over his "unclean" lips that are then cleansed by a coal from the altar fire. The call narrative of Isaiah is surprising in several ways, including the fact that it occurs in chapter 6 rather than the beginning of the book and that the mission he is given has a negative rather than positive role. For more discussion, see the Commentary section.

Natural Imagery

The book of Isaiah is notable for its incorporation of natural imagery within both its judgment and salvation oracles. The extent of this should be clear in the commentary section, as almost every part of the book includes some sort of ecological vision. God often illustrates the wickedness and punishment of Israel and Judah by using natural images of wilderness, unruly vineyards, and devastation. God's judgment itself is often pictured as flood or ravaging wildfire. On the other hand, the promised time of redemption and salvation will have profound ecological benefits, including harmony between carnivorous enemies and teeming agricultural fertility.

Symbolic Actions

Only Ezekiel surpasses Isaiah in the frequency and importance of symbolic actions. Isaiah fathers at least two, and perhaps three, children to serve as "signs" for the truth of his prophecy to Ahaz in 734 BCE. As with Hosea, the names of Israelite children are important, but Immanuel and Maher-shalal-hash-baz also function as "time stamps" to show that the foreign invasion will be over in two years. In addition to these symbolic actions, Isaiah is said to have walked around naked for *three years* to make the point that Egypt, Ethiopia, and Ashdod will not be able to stand against the Assyrian invasion of 715 BCE (Isa 20). Just as the prophet is naked, the prophecy goes, so shall the inhabitants of these nations be led naked and shamed into captivity.

Apocalyptic

Pure "apocalyptic literature" does not appear in Israel until the Hellenistic period of the fourth through second centuries BCE, but the ideas found there developed over a long period of time. Isaiah's visions of a redeemed community living in harmony and peace certainly influenced the developing apocalyptic vision of the future. However, as political realities became even more difficult, Isaiah's basic optimism devolves into a darker, dualistic outlook in which this world must be destroyed— wicked people with it—and replaced by a new heaven and a new earth. (Similar proto-apocalyptic thinking is found in Ezekiel, Joel, and Zechariah and is seen in full in the second century BCE text of Dan 7–12.) In Third Isaiah we find hints of apocalyptic thought (60:1-3; 65:17-25; 66:22-24). Also, chapters 24–27 have been described as Isaiah's "little apocalypse" and might date even later than Third Isaiah. These apocalyptic chapters certainly draw upon the earlier themes and motifs of Isaiah and should be seen as part of a larger continuum rather than separate from the book in which they are found.

Commentary

Isaiah 1–6

The first few oracles in Isaiah share language and theology with the book of Hosea. Isaiah begins with God's lament over wayward children who turn away from the source of their life and health and toward some corrupt replacement for God. Hosea uses this image of wayward children primarily with respect to religious idolatry and syncretism (i.e., incorporating foreign religious elements into their worship). Isaiah, though, seems more concerned with political alliances with foreigners and loss of Israel and Judah's distinctive identity as God's special possession. Isaiah 2:6-8 explicitly connects the veneration of idols with the reliance on foreigners.

Isaiah also expresses dissatisfaction with the people's efforts to appease God with rituals and sacrifices (1:12-17) while they continue to act unjustly, an idea that has appeared already in Amos and Hosea. God says that the people's prayers cannot be heard while their "hands are full of blood" (1:15b), but they may hope for mercy if they "learn to do good; seek justice, rescue the oppressed, defend the orphan, plead for the widow" (1:17). The political leaders are selfish and the judicial system corrupt, with the effect that vulnerable members of society cannot get justice (1:23; cf. Amos 5:12 and Mic 7:3). The connection between *justice* and *righteousness* is clear in the "song of the vineyard" in 5:1-10. In this passage Israel and Judah are pictured as God's vineyard, carefully prepared and empowered to provide the fruit of justice and righteousness. Using Hebrew puns, the prophet says that instead of justice the vineyard produces "bloodshed" and instead of righteousness "a cry" (5:7).

Now we see, even more than in Hosea, that God's judgment of this sinful people is part of a larger divine purpose. Isaiah 1:25-27 uses an industrial metaphor: God's purification is like the smelting of ore to create a pure and strong metal. Those who rebel against God will be destroyed, but those who repent in righteousness will form the basis of a newly created "faithful city." This is echoed in Isaiah 3:16–4:6, a description of how the luxurious women of Judah will be stricken and shamed ("instead of perfume there will be a stench," 3:24a) while the men are mostly killed in battle so that these humiliated women will be left husbandless. After this terrible period of degradation, the city will be once again made beautiful and pleasant, "once the Lord has washed away the filth" (4:4).

Indeed, as we shall see, Isaiah provides some of the most powerful images of redemption in the Bible, the first of which is in 2:2-4. In an excellent example of what scholars call *prophetic eschatology*, Isaiah looks far into the future to describe what God has in store beyond the present period of judgment and finds a powerful vision of reconciliation and universal inclusivism. He says that Jerusalem will be established as the most important city in the world (2:2); that from the temple God will preside over a world free from rivalry and warfare. Crafting language that still resonates with the Western religious imagination, Isaiah says that "they shall beat their swords into plowshares, and their spears into pruning hooks" (2:4b), bringing an end to all war and violence.

This breathtaking vision of peace and reconciliation expresses two of Isaiah's central theological affirmations: 1) God is the Lord of all history and guides international events for divine purposes, and 2) God's overall plan is to establish the kingdom of God—God's reign of justice and righteousness—throughout the whole world and not only in Israel or Judah. This vision of worldwide redemption is not exclusivist or pluralist but rather inclusivist; what God is doing upon Mount Zion will echo and reverberate to become the salvation of the whole world.

A common theme in First Isaiah is the corruption and decline of Israel and Judah's political and religious leadership. There are many references to corrupt priests, prophets, and princes, but none is as striking as his description of the anarchy that follows foreign invasion in Isaiah 3:1-15. The leaders have neglected their duties to judge and protect the poor and have instead oppressed and stolen from them. God asks sarcastically, "What do you mean by crushing my people, by grinding the face of the poor?" (3:15). The leaders have "misled" and "confused" the people so that any real leadership has completely vanished and they are ruled over by children and women (3:4, 12). Without good government, the people are free to oppress each other (3:5) and cannot find anyone who is even willing to try to govern them (3:6-7). Because of this, God presses a case against them, the *rib* lawsuit that we saw in Hosea 4. (For more on the corruption of Israel's leadership, see the discussion of Isa 28.)

Finally, we should say a few words about the remarkable "call narrative" in chapter 6, which is influenced by the architecture of the Jerusalem temple and Judean theology of God's abiding presence, as well as by the theophany tradition discussed in the section on Habakkuk 3. God is present in the temple and can be met there, but God is not contained or limited by that physical building. Therefore, Isaiah sees God "high and lofty," enthroned in the Holy of Holies, but "the hem of his robe filled the temple" (6:1). God is present there but also transcendent. The holiness of that sight initially makes Isaiah despair for his life, but an angel purifies his lips with a coal from the altar fire. Isaiah hears God ask for someone to be the divine messenger to the people, to which he responds famously, "Here am I; send me!" (6:8b). Like Moses in Exodus 3, this theophanic vision of God leads to the prophet's call and commissioning.

Isaiah's commission instructions in vv. 9-10 are unexpected and often overlooked in readings of this passage. God does not send Isaiah to warn the people in the hope that they may turn from their ways and be saved. He is not even sent as one who announces the inexorable doom that is on its way, as was Amos. More disturbingly, Isaiah is part of God's punishment plan; he is told to "make the mind of this people dull, and stop their ears, and shut their eyes" (6:10). Why? So that there will be no chance for them to repent and so be saved from the coming destruction. As we will see in Isaiah 28:13 (and was evidenced in the story of Micaiah ben Imlah in 1 Kgs 22), when people refuse to listen to prophetic warnings, God may cause prophecy to cease or even corrupt the prophetic message itself in order to seal the divine judgment.

Isaiah is astonished at this difficult assignment, asking, "How long, O Lord?" (6:11). God says that he should confuse and confound the people "until cities lie waste" and "vast is the emptiness in the midst of the land" (6:11-12). Terrible destruction and exile are coming, and at this late stage there is nothing the people can do to change it. Isaiah is not only a witness to this bleak situation, but part of God's unfolding judgment. As difficult as this passage is to accept, it is important to note that in other passages Isaiah speaks plainly about what God is doing and how his listeners should turn back to God. The harsh edge of Isaiah's commissioning reinforces the seriousness of the situation, but it is only part of Isaiah's larger theological canvas.

Isaiah 7–12

Chapters 7–12 form the heart of First Isaiah and are crucial to understanding the overall perspective of the book. Chapters 7–8 address the time of the Syro-Ephraimite crisis in 734 BCE; chapter 10 contains an extended reflection on the nature of God's "dual agency" with unwitting human agents of judgment; chapters 9 and 11 contain the most famous "messianic" predictions in the prophetic corpus. Our discussion will begin with chapter 10 and then work through from the start of chapter 7.

Isaiah 10:5-19

We have previously discussed Isaiah 10:5-19 as an example of shifting first-person voices. It begins with God speaking about the king of Assyria, then shifts in vv. 8-14 to the actual voice of the Assyrian conqueror. This is a "quotation" only in the rhetorical sense, of course. The prophet presents these words in the king's voice in order to heighten the dramatic power of the passage. The last five verses switch to the voice of the prophet himself, interpreting the exchange that has just passed between God and the king.

The meaning of this oracle is that God sends the king of Assyria to accomplish the divine will of judgment on wicked nations. Here, God is the Lord of history who directs all international events regardless of which nations are involved. The Assyrian king has no knowledge of this divine purpose, however, and boasts that his power has enabled him to gather up nations like eggs in unprotected nests (10:14). He reasons that since he has had no trouble with any nation or city before, why would Jerusalem and Samaria prove to be any different? The "idols" of Judah will not be able to stand against him and his powerful army (10:9-11). Isaiah says that God has a larger plan that involves the ultimate punishment of the Assyrians as well. Because the king has been so boastful and violent, God will punish the Assyrian king "when the Lord has finished all his work on Mount Zion" (i.e., Jerusalem, 10:12).

The underlying assumption in this complex prophecy is that God and the Assyrian king are tied together in a "dual agency." God decides to use the king for divine purposes, but the king also makes his own decisions and is responsible for his actions. A similar perspective can be found in the actions of the Egyptian pharaoh in Exodus 7–15 and in God's use of the violent Babylonians in Habakkuk. The Assyrian king is a tool of God yet still answerable for his arrogant actions. As the prophet says, "Shall an ax vaunt itself over the one who wields it?" (10:15a).

Isaiah 7–8

In 734 BCE Jerusalem was attacked by a coalition of the Aramean king Rezin and the Israelite king Pekah, an event known in scholarship as the Syro-Ephraimite crisis. Their goal was to remove Ahaz from the throne and replace him with someone who would cooperate with their regional alliance against the Assyrian invasion. The prophecies that address this situation are important from a theological point of view and also provide a fascinating glimpse into the politically fraught nature of prophecy.

According to Isaiah, God does not want Ahaz to worry about his position on the throne but to trust in God's protection of the city and of the Davidic line (Isaiah's view is informed by Zion theology, discussed in the "Theological Traditions" section). He says, "Take heed, be quiet, do not fear" (7:4), but these words put Ahaz in a political predicament. God evidently wants him to do nothing—not to join the Syro-Ephraimite coalition and not to rely upon any other foreign power to come to his rescue. God decrees that the attack on Jerusalem will not be successful and that neither of the invading nations will survive the Assyrian invasion (7:7-9). The key for Ahaz is to "stand firm in faith" or else he "shall not stand at all" (7:9). In order to reinforce this message,

Isaiah brings his son Shear-jashub (which means "a remnant shall return") with him to address the king as a "sign" of the prophecy. There are several options for interpreting that name in this situation, but one strong possibility is that it means that only a remnant of the attacking army will return northward.

Assuming that Ahaz decides to do nothing, the natural question would be for how long. How long would he be able to maintain a neutral position in the midst of this international crisis? This is where the other two children in this passage come into play. In Isaiah 8:1-4 God tells Isaiah to conceive a child with a prophetess and to name the child Maher-shalal-hash-baz, or "the spoil speeds, the prey hastens." The reason for this is to serve as a "time stamp" on the prophecy: before the child can say simple words like "mommy," the nations of Aram and Israel will be plundered by Assyria. Adding up the gestation period and the normal age of speech development, Ahaz must hold out for only two years or so. If he gives in to pressure from either Israel or Assyria, the consequences could be much longer and severe. So if Isaiah's prophecy is correct, then it makes more political sense to wait for the Lord's deliverance.

The second of the three children in this passage is the most familiar and controversial: Immanuel. In Isaiah 7:10-17, Isaiah invites Ahaz to ask God for a sign, and Ahaz refuses in a false show of piety. The real reason that Ahaz does not want a sign is because it would force him into doing what Isaiah has said, namely nothing, especially if the prophecy became public. In frustration Isaiah says that "the LORD himself will give you a sign," followed by the words "the young woman is with child and shall bear a son, and shall name him Immanuel" (7:14). This passage is quoted by the angel to Joseph, the father of Jesus, and has been read by Christians primarily as a prophecy of the birth of the Messiah (Matt 1:23). Looking at the whole of Isaiah 7–8, however, we see how this prophesied birth fits into its historical and literary context. The birth of Immanuel functions in the same way as that of Maher-shalal-hash-baz in the next chapter. By the time Immanuel is weaned (i.e., eating curds and honey) and develops a sense of right and wrong, "the land before whose two kings you are in dread will be deserted" (7:15-16). The focus of the prophecy is on the timing of the child's birth and early childhood, with respect to the attack on Jerusalem by the Israelites and Assyrians. This time stamp is a bit more open-ended than that of the third child, but seems to be within the same two-year window. The verbal form used for pregnancy in v. 14 is ambiguous: the woman could either already be pregnant or just about to become pregnant. Also, although Matthew 1:23 interprets this as a miraculous conception, there is nothing in Isaiah 7 itself to suggest that the woman has become pregnant while still a virgin. The term that is translated as "virgin" in the King James Version and the New International Version is *almah*, which means "young woman." If Isaiah's intent were to say that the woman has (or will) become pregnant through divine means, we would expect him to be more clear about it.

Finally, it is not clear who the woman is or whose child this will be. There are three basic options. One argument is that since Shear-jashub and Maher-shalal-hash-baz are both Isaiah's children, then Immanuel should be Isaiah's child as well. A second possibility, which happens to be the traditional Jewish interpretation, is that the woman is the wife of Ahaz, and the boy to be born is Hezekiah, the next king of Judah who inspired great hopes in the late eighth century BCE. The third option is to interpret the woman as Mary and the baby as Jesus, following the New Testament interpretation of Matthew 1. As discussed, the natural interpretation is to situate the text in the eighth century BCE, not hundreds of years later. However, it is entirely appropriate for Christians to read this text in more than one direction, both historically and, in retrospect, theologically. For more on this argument, see the section on the prophets and the New Testament in the Conclusion. Similar issues pertain to the next two chapters to be discussed.

Isaiah 9, 11

Two of the most familiar passages in Isaiah, at least during the Advent season, are found in chapters 9 and 11. Isaiah 9:2-7 and 11:1-9 are "messianic" predictions that resonate through both Jewish and Christian traditions, the latter most majestically in Handel's *Messiah*. As with the Immanuel prophecy, it is appropriate for Christian readers to connect these texts to the story of Jesus, as the New Testament does. Nevertheless, these prophecies have meaning for the prophet and for his audience in his own time and place. What did these oracles mean in their original context? They predict the coming of a king who will restore Judah's fortunes, deliver it from foreign oppressors, and bring about a time of peace, prosperity, and health beyond reckoning. As such, they are part of a larger "messianic" tradition that intensifies as one moves toward the postexilic prophets and apocalyptic movements.

Isaiah 9:2-3 says that a "great light" has illuminated the people in their darkness, leading to rejoicing. The source of such joy is that God has broken "the bar across their shoulders, the rod of their oppressor" (9:4), which refers to the invading armies whose boots and bloody uniforms will now be used as fuel for the fire (9:5). Intriguingly, the terms used for "tramping boots" are related to the Assyrian words for high-laced boots. With this word choice the prophet calls to mind the very real and terrifying Assyrian invasion. But, he says, this threat is coming to an end because "a child has been born" who has been given authority and who will rule over a renewed, peaceful kingdom from the throne of David (9:6-7). If we regard this passage as original to the eighth-century BCE prophet Isaiah, then it may be that this poem, as well as the one in Isaiah 11, celebrates the birth or the inauguration of Ahaz's son Hezekiah. Second Kings 18–20 and 2 Chronicles 29–31 reveal that Hezekiah's reign was one of renewed hopes for Judean independence.

Readers who are accustomed to reading this passage as a description of Jesus will wonder how the highly elevated language in vv. 6-7 could be a description of a human king. The NRSV translates the titles as "Wonderful Counselor, Mighty God, Everlasting Father, Prince of Peace," which sound divine indeed, especially with the capital letters. How could Hezekiah be described like this? One clue is to see how other cultures in the ancient world describe their kings. It is common for kings to assume royal titles that appear to us to be rather over the top. These epithets emphasize the king's role as guardian and protector of his people, the one who establishes the kingdom in wisdom and piece. That part is plain enough, but what about "Mighty God"? There are two points to consider here. First, even in Israel it is assumed that the king has a close connection to God, even to the point of being the agent of divine power in the human world. Recall that in Psalm 2 God says that David has become God's "son" (v. 7), itself a passage that takes on Christian meaning in later centuries. Second, the Hebrew phrase translated "Mighty God" is not as clear as it may sound in the English translation. The phrase *el gibbor* is an interesting construction of the generic term "god" (not the more common name of God, *elohim*) and an adjective that refers to military might. Taken together, they suggest that the king has been endowed with godlike military powers, a very common idea in the ancient world. Therefore, it is plausible to read this text in its original context as an expression of hope that God will elevate the Davidic line to its rightful place.

Isaiah 11:1-9 covers much of the same ground but with even more creative imagery. It begins by evoking the ancient tradition that the king is responsible for establishing justice and righteousness in his realm. The acts of judging fairly, protecting the poor, and punishing the wicked are all consonant with the prophets' application of covenantal traditions to Israelite society (11:3-4). Verses 6-9 present a lovely vision of peace and security: "the wolf shall live with the lamb, the leopard shall lie down with the kid, the calf and the lion and the fatling together, and a little child shall lead them" (11:6) and concluding with "they will not hurt or destroy on all my holy mountain" (11:9).

Ultimately, both of these texts describe the coming of the kingdom of God, defined as the place where God is honored as king and where God's justice and righteousness are universal. God will establish this kingdom through the work of the anointed king, the messiah. In later Jewish and Christian tradition this messianic theology develops in diverse ways, including the spiritualized interpretation of Jesus as the "crucified" Messiah (1 Cor 1:23).

Finally, no reading of Isaiah 7–12 is complete without reading the beautiful expressions of hope and redemption in Isaiah 11:10–12:6. These passages probably date to the exilic period since they predict the gathering of the inhabitants of both Israel and Judah who have been dispersed (11:12). However, it is possible that the eighth-century prophet Isaiah here looks beyond the current crisis to something better in the distant future (cf. Isa 2:2-4). Notice the hallmarks of this glorious and blessed future: Israel and Judah will no longer be rivals but will cooperate in subduing their regional rivals (11:13); the people will turn toward God in trust and gratitude (12:1); and God's acts of salvation will be proclaimed among all the world's nations so that the name of God will be exalted (12:4-6).

Isaiah 13–27

This large middle section of First Isaiah includes texts that likely originated during the eighth century BCE but were edited during later periods. Chapters 13–23 contain "oracles against the nations" and some interesting reflections on God's larger purposes within world events. Chapters 24–27 are known as the "little apocalypse" of Isaiah and most likely date to the postexilic period. This passage has much in common with the apocalyptic literature of Daniel and Joel and will be discussed only briefly.

Isaiah 13–23

These oracles address a wide range of foreign powers and international issues. It is tempting to connect these texts with particular historical events, but these efforts at historical identification must always remain tentative due to the simple fact that the oracles do not have historical prologues and were often edited to address later events as well. For example, Isaiah 13:1 says that this is an oracle "concerning Babylon." It describes in great detail the violent destruction of that city and the misery of its population. Verse 17 attributes the destruction of Babylon to "the Medes," an Iranian kingdom that was active in the eighth and seventh centuries BCE. We know that the Medes were the allies of Babylon in the overthrow of Nineveh in 612 BCE (see the discussion of Nahum) and that during Hezekiah's time the Babylonians were potential Judean allies against the Assyrians (cf. Isa 39:1). So was this oracle a very precocious denunciation of Babylon during the eighth century, or was it written during the exile in the sixth century to describe Babylon's actual demise? As Isaiah 45:1 recognizes, the fall of Babylon was at the hands of the Persians, not the Medes. It seems that the oracle was originally directed against Assyria in the eighth century and was later applied to Babylon as the text was revised in the late exilic period.

This oracular reuse is important because chapter 14 shows the same kind of ambiguity: it describes the downfall of a great king, identified as the "king of Babylon" (14:4). However, the language in the oracle fits well within the time of Isaiah of Jerusalem, and 14:25 specifically mentions the Assyrians. So it seems likely that here we again see an original Isaianic oracle against Assyria in the eighth century being reapplied to Babylon at the end of the sixth. What makes chapter 14 more important, however, is that the description of the king's downfall was interpreted in the Christian tradition to be that of Satan's rebellion against God and subsequent expulsion from heaven. Verse 11 says that the king's "pomp is brought down to Sheol," which was identified as hell in the Christian tradition. Moreover, 14:12 taunts the king: "How you are fallen from heaven, O Day Star, son of Dawn," which the King James Version translates as "O Lucifer, son of the morning," following the Latin rendering of "Day Star," *lucifer*. In the Christian tradition, especially John Milton's *Paradise Lost*, this "Lucifer" is identified as Satan, this passage being the history of his fall from heaven.

Since we have seen that the prophecy originally described a certain king and was reworked to address a later king, it is not surprising that the interpretation of this text would continue to evolve. Notice, however, that vv. 16-20 clearly describe the physical death and ignominious burial of a disgraced human king. It is important to recognize that although this text may be quoted in discussions about Satan and hell, it should first be interpreted metaphorically within its historical context. The description of the king's arrogance (e.g., "'I will ascend to heaven; I will raise my throne above the stars of God,'" 14:13) might sound too grand for a human figure, but ancient kings most certainly did describe themselves in such high terms. In any case the quotation is meant to be sarcastic and not something he could actually accomplish.

After the texts concerning Babylon/Assyria, the oracles address the Philistines (14:21-32), Moab (chs. 15–16), Aram (ch. 17), Ethiopia (ch. 18), Egypt (ch. 19), Ashdod (ch. 20), and Tyre (ch. 23). Different approaches are reflected in these oracles. The Philistines are warned not to be overconfident now that Israel has been destroyed by the Assyrians and that their devastation is coming as well (14:29). The prophet laments the destruction of Moab and expresses concern for its dead and refugee citizens, calling for other nations to shelter them (15:3-4). In 16:11 God says, "My heart throbs like a harp for Moab, and my very soul for Kir-heres." This oracle has been updated, however, with a more negative view of Moab (16:13-14), saying that the "past" oracle of lament for Moab has been changed to one of judgment: "In three years, like the years of a hired worker, the glory of Moab will be brought into contempt." We find a similar update in 23:13-18, saying that Babylon, not Assyria, was the actual agent of Tyre's destruction. The description of the destruction of Damascus (17:1-3) may have originally described the fall of that city in 732 BCE, the end of the Syro-Ephraimite coalition previously discussed in chapters 7–8. The prophet moves from the fall of Damascus to the coming invasion of Israel for its part in that attack on Jerusalem (17:4). Isaiah holds out hope that this might cause Israel to turn back to God (17:7-8), but this optimism is quickly replaced by certainty of their coming judgment (17:10-14).

God's Servants, the Prophets

The reflection on the nations of Ethiopia and Egypt is particularly interesting because they express the budding universalism that is a major theme in Isaiah. These two northern African nations were chief rivals to the Assyrians, and occasionally they provided hope to Judah in her attempts to remain independent (see Isa 30–31). Chapter 18 shows respectful admiration for the Ethiopians, "a nation tall and smooth" (v. 2) and predicts that in the end they shall bring offerings to the Lord in Jerusalem (v. 7). With regard to Egypt, the prophet predicts that God will stir them up in confusion and incite a brutal civil war, which will devastate and humble them (19:2-3, 14). They will ultimately come to be afraid of Judah and its God (19:16-17) and worship God in the heart of Egypt (19:19). The Lord will punish Egypt, "striking and healing," but "they will return to the LORD, and he will listen to their supplications and heal them" (19:22). This is an astonishing move for the prophet and reveals the development of a more inclusive and universal view of God's action in the world. Here, we see God as the Lord of history, maneuvering international events not only for the good of Judah but also for the redemption of other peoples of the world. This oracle ends with the idea that Egypt and Assyria will be united socially and religiously and that Israel will be a "third" with them, "a blessing in the midst of the earth" (19:23-25).

Finally, chapters 21 and 22 include some of the most thoughtful descriptions of the violent chaos of the period. In three oracles addressed to the "wilderness of the sea," the "desert plain," and the "valley of vision," the prophet describes the anxiety and tumult of military invasion. He is moved with anguish (21:3), his mind reels with horror (21:4), and he weeps bitter tears for "the destruction of my beloved people" (22:4). The prophet's stern condemnation of the people was not without sorrow at how Israel and Judah's situation had turned.

ISAIAH

Isaiah 24–27

As the prophetic tradition developed during the eighth to the fifth centuries BCE, its literary nature and theological perspective changed. In Isaiah 2:2-4, for instance, we find what may be called a "prophetic eschatology," a description of the prophet's final vision for the world. Isaiah looks forward and sees a time of completion in which God's kingdom will be established on earth, a time of justice and righteousness and reconciliation among all peoples. This is a fundamentally optimistic outlook that expects the future to share basic continuity with the present. In other words, normal time will pass until, eventually, inhabitants of this world will see the fulfillment of God's final purposes.

Later, especially moving into the Hellenistic period of Greek rule during the fourth through second centuries BCE, this optimistic prophetic eschatology developed into a more pessimistic, "apocalyptic eschatology." In Daniel and other early Jewish apocalyptic books, we see a vision of the future that is discontinuous with the present: God will finally destroy this world and create a new one, a blessed realm for the few who remain during this present age. The world is caught in a vast struggle between good and evil, and those who are persecuted for their faith are rewarded by God. Daniel 12 predicts their physical resurrection from the dead, a rare reference to resurrection in the Hebrew Bible.

Isaiah 24–27 has more in common with this apocalyptic imagination than with Isaiah of Jerusalem. There are certainly points of connection, but the overall genre of the text seems to be "apocalypse" rather than that of judgment oracle. The world will be "utterly laid waste and utterly despoiled" (24:3). This is not the effect of warfare but rather God's heavenly assault on the earth and its wicked inhabitants (24:19-22). Those who are oppressed in this evil age will experience vindication and be rewarded for their patient waiting (25:9). There is even hope for the physical resurrection of the dead (26:19), perhaps with Daniel the only such prediction in the Hebrew Bible. Notice, however, that these apocalyptic ideas end with a prediction of universal worship in Jerusalem, a sentiment we find in Isaiah 2:2-4 and in the oracles concerning Ethiopia, Egypt, and Assyria. Though chapters 24–27 likely date to much later than the eighth-century prophet, this apocalyptic section intentionally draws upon the Isaiah tradition, incorporating motifs and images from the earlier period. This majestic expression of hope in God's final victory over the powers of injustice and oppression calls on God's people to remain faithful and waiting.

Isaiah 28–39

The final section of First Isaiah includes a few oracles that date to the time of the original prophet, a few that likely date to a later time, and a whole section of historical material that is duplicated from 2 Kings. It is a complex mix of traditions, and we will focus here on the most important early texts.

Isaiah 28

The beginning of this prophecy addresses "the drunkards of Ephraim," a reference to the northern kingdom of Israel (28:1). Thus, we find ourselves again in the midst of the chaotic final years of Israel before the destruction of Samaria in 722 BCE. This oracle places the blame for that catastrophe squarely upon Israel's leadership, including priests, prophets, princes, and the rich. Isaiah pictures them as engaging in a lavish party with fine wine and rich food, unaware that they are soon to be destroyed as in a storm flood (28:2). He draws upon the image of a "garland," a decorative headpiece that the partiers wear but that will be thrown down and trampled under foot (28:3). In its place God will become the "garland of glory" for the faithful remnant (28:5).

What is most striking about this passage is its description of the depravity of the Israelite leaders and how that has compromised their ability to fulfill their responsibilities to the people. They are so drunk that they stagger around in a room where every surface is covered in vomit (28:8). We realize quickly, however, that this drunkenness is not only physical but also spiritual. Because they are so confused and dull, God will respond by speaking to them "with stammering lip" (28:11). They will hear the prophetic word as a series of unintelligible sounds, the equivalent of "blah, blah, blah" (28:10). This recalls the commissioning of Isaiah, in which he is commanded to "make the mind of this people dull," to confuse even more an already confused people. Compare here the statement in Isaiah 29:10 that "the Lord has poured out upon you a spirit of deep sleep; he has closed your eyes, you prophets." The blinding of the prophets and obscuring of the divine word serve as a prelude to God's establishment of justice and righteousness, the leadership's failed responsibility. The prophet compares this to a cleansing and destructive floodwater (28:17; cf. Amos 5:24 and Isa 8:7).

The overwhelming power of God is emphasized in chapter 29 with the vision of an attack on Jerusalem, called "Ariel," which may mean "altar hearth." God promises to "besiege" the city, which will force the people to hide in deep underground shelters (29:3). Then, however, the oracle shifts to a vision of Jerusalem being attacked by a host of foreign armies (29:5-8). In response, God appears in a theophany of thunder and earthquake and reduces all the attackers to nothing. Such a powerful God is Jerusalem's only hope during these times.

One of the major problems in Israel seems to have been their attempt to make an alliance with the Egyptians and other nations in order to protect themselves from Assyria, an alliance that Isaiah calls a "covenant with death" (28:18). Isaiah complains about Israel being overrun with foreigners in chapter 2 and, as we will see, is dismissive of the ability of Egypt to stand against Assyria in chapters 30 and 31. Indeed, Israel's (and Judah's) only hope is to trust in God, which concludes with Isaiah's words to Ahaz that he should "stand firm in faith" (7:9; cf. 30:15). Instead of attending to this hard message, the people command the prophets to "speak to us smooth things, prophesy illusions" (30:10), and put their trust in lies rather than in the way of God.

Thinking themselves clever, they try to hide their plans from the Lord (29:15), "carrying out a plan," but against God's will (30:1), in their attempts to make a protective alliance with Egypt (31:2). They are evidently impressed with the power of Egypt's army and horses (30:16; 31:1), but when God brings judgment, "the helper will stumble, and the one helped will fall" (31:3b). However, if the people will trust in God, they can be saved from the Assyrians through God's deliverance (31:8). Isaiah 30:27-33 narrates an astonishing scene that pictures God putting the king of Assyria to death in a kind of sacrificial ritual. It is a theophany scene in which God appears in smoke and fire and beats the Assyrian with a rod until he dies and is burned upon the "tophet," a ritual place near Jerusalem associated with human sacrifice (translated "burning place"; Isa 30:33).

The prophet expresses hope that when God finally delivers Judah from the Assyrian crisis, they will respond with repentance and trust, and God will restore their fortunes (29:22-24; 30:18-26). Isaiah 32:17-18 says that if the people turn back to righteousness, they will find peace, quietness, and security. This trust in God's power to rescue Jerusalem is at the heart of Isaiah's "Zion theology." This perspective was powerfully reinforced in 701 BCE when the Assyrian king Sennacherib invaded Judah after Hezekiah's rebellion against Assyria. This invasion is the central focus of Isaiah 36–39 and is narrated as well in 2 Kings 18–20. When Sennacherib's army was camped outside the city, Hezekiah quickly gave him everything of value in the city as tribute (2 Kgs 18:14-16). This might explain why Sennacherib did not destroy the city and depose Hezekiah, which one would have expected him to do. Whereas Sennacherib boasts in his annals of destroying many rebellious cities and towns, he admits that he accepted tribute and left Hezekiah on the throne. Was he unable to breach Jerusalem's defenses? An alternate explanation is offered in Isaiah 37:33-38, in which an angel of God kills 185,000 Assyrian soldiers during the night, prompting Sennacherib to abandon his attack. Regardless of what happened, the Judeans interpreted their survival as God's rescue of the city. Such

Isaiah

confidence in God's protection of Jerusalem resonated deeply in the tradition and finally came to be interpreted by Jeremiah as false confidence and self-deception (Jer 7:1-15).

Isaiah 40–55

Isaiah 40–55 is known by scholars as "Deutero-Isaiah," or "Second Isaiah." As discussed in the "Historical Context" section, it appears to derive from late in the exilic period, probably around 550 BCE, just before the victory of the Persian leader Cyrus the Great over Babylon. Since this book focuses primarily on the preexilic prophets, we will examine the aspects of Second Isaiah that draw upon and extend the ideas of First Isaiah. The prophets and scribes responsible for Second Isaiah probably had access to Isaiah's original oracles and saw themselves as keepers of that tradition.

Chapter 40 immediately shifts the tone and perspective of the book. Rather than the heavy focus on judgment in First Isaiah, the first words of 40:1 are "Comfort, O comfort my people." The people have been punished—even *doubly* punished—for their sins and are about to see the glory of the Lord revealed in their salvation (40:5). From this point the book features a series of oracles that reflect on the nature and goodness of God and call on the people to rejoice and move forward with thanksgiving and confidence.

Whereas Isaiah 1–39 develops a theology of God as the Lord of history, Second Isaiah takes that idea even further, emphasizing God as the Lord of all creation. The book draws a strong contrast between God and the human world. People are like "grass" that withers compared with the eternal word of God (40:7-8). Compared with God's power and wisdom, nations are like "a drop from a bucket" (40:15; notice the correct version of the common phrase "drop in a bucket"). God sits above the creation, and its inhabitants are "like grasshoppers" (40:22).

The Creator God is Israel's hope in the midst of struggle and also reveals the worthlessness of human idols. Second Isaiah contains the most biting critiques of "iconic" worship in all of Scripture. Isaiah 44:9-20 describes the process of an artisan's creation of an object for worship. He burns half of the wood for a fire and for cooking dinner and then uses the rest to make an idol, to which he bows down in worship, saying, "Save me, for you are my god!" (44:17). Echoing Isaiah 6:10, the prophet says that the people who rely on such empty images are blind and uncomprehending, unable to realize that the image is "a fraud" (44:20).

When God says in 44:6 "I am the first and I am the last; besides me there is no god," this is the earliest clear expression of philosophical monotheism in the Bible (cf. 45:22; 48:12-13). The first commandment in Exodus 20:3 says, "You shall have no other gods before me" but stops short of denying that any other such gods might exist in the world. Israel's early henotheism, meaning their exclusive worship of one God, transforms into pure monotheism as a result of the exile experience. While in a foreign land surrounded by polytheists, they come to the conclusion that if God is the Lord of history, then no other gods must exist. God alone, the only God, could accomplish these things that were happening.

God's power over creation is not used for destructive or capricious ends. Rather, God "strengthens the powerless" (40:29), which is a comfort to those who need such a strong ally (cf. 44:24-25; 45:7; 46:9). God's plans for redeeming Israel flow through the efforts of Cyrus, the Persian leader who defeated the Babylonians in the middle of the sixth century BCE. Isaiah 42:2 says that God has "roused" Cyrus and has delivered up nations to him (cf. 41:25). In 44:28 Isaiah calls Cyrus the "shepherd" of God, and in 45:1 God's "anointed" (Hebrew, "messiah"). Even though Cyrus does not know what role he plays (45:4), God has opened doors for Cyrus and "armed" him for rescuing Israel (45:5). The fact that Cyrus is following his own desires while God uses him for a larger purpose makes Cyrus the twin of the Assyrian king in Isaiah 10:5. However, there is no hint that Cyrus will be judged in the same way that the Assyrian king is punished for his arrogance.

There is repeated emphasis in these chapters on the confidence and optimism that Israel should feel as a rescued and redeemed community. God has honored the covenant agreement with Jacob and therefore tells Israel, "Do not be afraid, for I am your God" (42:10), and "I have called you by name, you are mine" (42:25). God promises to help Israel, to provide for the poor and thirsty (42:7), to gather the exiles from both east and west (43:5-7), and to remember no longer their sin of turning from God (43:22-25; 48:9-11; 54:4-8). Therefore, as Israelites leave Babylon for Jerusalem, they should shout with joy and proclaim the redemption of Israel by God (48:20). They will be helped in their rebuilding by other nations and kings (49:22-23), and in return God's teaching and justice shall be "a light to the peoples" (51:4-6). The descriptions of Israel's blessed life after the exile (e.g., 51:11; 55:12–13) resonate with the eschatological passage in 2:2-4. Clearly, the prophet expects that life after this restoration will be a major step in the coming of God's kingdom.

Finally, notice the series of "Servant Songs" in which an individual is described as serving God faithfully in the midst of difficulties: 42:1-4; 45:5-7; 49:1-6; 50:4-9; 52:13–53:12. One common interpretation of these songs is that the "servant" is Israel itself, especially in its relationship to the nations. As God redeems Israel from suffering, so that redemption will do good for the world at large. It is also possible that the servant is the prophet himself, in his tasks of delivering God's word and of mediating between God and the people. The last song in this sequence is the passage of the "Suffering Servant," which is quoted in Acts 8:32-35 as a reference to the innocent suffering of Jesus, and this has been the dominant interpretation in the Christian tradition.

Isaiah 56–66

Isaiah 56–66 is called by scholars "Trito-Isaiah" or "Third Isaiah." Some argue that all of chapters 40–66 should be considered one section, but clues within the final eleven chapters suggest that this last section may date to the time *after* the Judeans were returned to Jerusalem in 538 BCE. There are references to ritual activity and sacrifices taking place in

Jerusalem, which implies that they have at least begun rebuilding the temple but have probably not finished it (64:11; which they do in 515 BCE). There are also references to city ruins, struggles with hunger, political chaos, and many yet-to-be-returned exiles, which implies a setting early in the restoration process.

One of the basic issues that face the returning Judean exiles is how to reconstruct their communal identity and on what basis. In Ezra 9–10, there arises a conflict over so-called "foreign wives," which results in the banishment of women and children who do not share Israel's "holy seed" (Ezra 9:2). There is a hint that these women are a religious threat to the community, but the only specific charge brought against them has to do with their parentage. Third Isaiah is on the other side of this cultural debate. In chapter 56 the prophet says that two groups of people are welcome among the people of God even though they have been prohibited by the laws of Deuteronomy 23:1-6. In vv. 3-5 eunuchs who worship God and keep the Sabbath are welcome in the community and will find within it a sense of identity beyond simple family ties. Further, vv. 6-7 say that foreigners who love God and keep the covenant will find their sacrifices and offerings accepted on the Jerusalem altar. Thus, Third Isaiah draws communal boundary markers on the basis of covenant keeping and worship of God. Anyone who joins with the Israelites in serving God is welcome. This sense of inclusiveness resonates as well with two other postexilic texts: the story of Ruth, the Moabite woman who was faithful to her Israelite mother-in-law and became the great-grandmother of David; and the story of Jonah, the prophet who discovers that God can have compassion and mercy even on Israel's bitter enemies.

The prophet extends this idea to suggest that God is in the midst of a larger plan of redemption that encompasses nations other than Israel. In 56:8 God says of Israel, "I will gather others to them besides those already gathered." We see a similar idea in the repeated notion that the nations will support Israel in her restoration and will then be blessed by God through Israel (60:3, 12; 66:18-21). Isaiah 61:5-9 is the most striking example of this, saying that nations that help Israel will receive "an everlasting covenant" with God, and everyone will know they have been blessed by the Lord.

The second major theme in Third Isaiah is the need for justice and righteousness in order for the emerging community to flourish. Several texts describe the injustice and wickedness rampant in the community. There are all kinds of abominable religious practices (65:1-11), including libations to other gods and child sacrifice (57:1-9; cf. 66:1-4). The people have corrupted the court system and promoted lies (59:2-4) and look only to their own ends rather than those of the poor and needy (58:1-4). Isaiah 58 contains one of the most memorable calls to true justice in the Bible. The people have been performing fasts and praying for God's help, with no effect. The prophet sarcastically describes their fasting (58:5) and then says what kind of fast God desires: to loose the bonds of injustice, free the oppressed, feed the hungry, shelter the homeless, and clothe the naked (58:6-9). Isaiah 61:1-2 says as well that God has proclaimed good news to the oppressed, liberty to captives, and comfort to mourners, a text quoted by Jesus about himself in Luke 4.

Isaiah emphasizes that those who persist in wickedness will be destroyed, but those who are humble and contrite will be forgiven and restored to health (58:9-12; 59:20-21; 65:11-14; 66:1-4). Chapter 63 contains a striking first-person description of God marching out as a divine warrior, bringing vengeance on the wicked. It begins with an image of God crushing grapes in a wine press in "wrath," a text that was used in "The Battle Hymn of the Republic," in which God is "trampling out the vintage where the grapes of wrath are stored," and referenced as well in John Steinbeck's novel *The Grapes of Wrath*. The prophet recognizes that the people are still unclean and have turned away from God in apathy (64:6-7) but asks God to have pity on the people, to remember that "we are all your people" (64:9b) and that Zion still lies in ruins and the temple destroyed (64:10-11). God's response is that all who reject God will be punished harshly ("I will destine you to the sword," 65:12), but those who serve God will prosper and rejoice

(65:13-16). Jerusalem will become like a mother, comforting and nursing her children (66:12-14), so people will know that God is with them. In a reference to the vision in Isaiah 11:6-9, Isaiah 65:25 promises that the wolf and lamb will live together, the lion will be a vegetarian, and the snake will eat dust, quoting Isaiah 11:9: "They shall not hurt or destroy on all my holy mountain."

Finally, the descriptions of the blessed life beginning in Jerusalem bear the stamp of the developing apocalyptic tradition. God is about to create "new heavens and a new earth" (65:17) and begin to establish what will become known as the kingdom of God. There is a strong contrast between the darkness of the world and the light of God's glory that shines over Israel (60:1-3). Indeed, the sun and moon will no longer be the main source of brightness; the Lord will shine over them (60:19-20; cf. Rev 21:23). In this blessed community there will be health and long life (65:20), freedom from oppression and slavery (65:21), and an end to all violence and killing. The book ends with a second mention of the "the new heavens and the new earth" (66:22) and the contrast between the righteous who live with God and those who will be killed and cast where the "worm shall not die" and the "fire shall not be quenched" (66:24) a text used by Jesus in Mark 9:48 to refer to hell. By the end of Isaiah, then, we find ourselves beginning the transition from prophetic to apocalyptic perspectives.

Chapter 4

Micah

Introduction

Micah is the last of the four eighth-century BCE prophets in the Bible. Amos and Hosea address the northern kingdom of Israel while Isaiah and Micah are active in Jerusalem and Judah, the southern kingdom. For both Isaiah and Micah, however, the events transpiring in Israel are of central importance to the present and future of Judah. Given the long rivalry between Israel and Judah, one might expect the Judeans to take a certain satisfaction in Israel's subjugation by Assyria. Once Ahaz becomes a vassal of the Assyrians in 734 BCE, Judah is not in any immediate danger, so it would be tempting to see God's judgment on Israel as just desserts and leave it at that.

For both Isaiah and Micah, however, the sins that have led to Israel's destruction are present in Judah. Will God allow Judah to be destroyed like its northern kindred? Micah emphasizes that just as Judah has the same sin as Israel, it will receive the same punishment (3:9-12). Its only hope is to "walk in the name of the LORD our God" (4:5).

The book of Micah does not only address the eighth-century BCE context, however. Later additions during the exile extend Micah's oracles by incorporating promises of restoration, forgiveness, and peace. Thus, Micah in its final form is structurally similar to Amos, Hosea, and Isaiah. It is more tightly presented than those others, however, and develops several unique images. It is most known for the often-quoted verse in 6:8, but that line is only a summary of the prophet's larger, compelling vision.

Historical Context

Micah of Moresheth is a Judean prophet whose ministry overlapped with that of Isaiah of Jerusalem near the end of the eighth century BCE. The superscription says that he is active during the time of Jotham, Ahaz, and Hezekiah, which is more or less identical to the dating of Isaiah. Micah's understanding of the historical situation is similar to that of Isaiah, and one of Isaiah's most familiar oracles (Isa 2:2-4) even finds its way into the text of Micah (4:1-3). The books of Isaiah and Micah are thus closely connected in history and theology.

Moresheth was a small town near Lachish, southeast of Jerusalem. Lachish is most notable in ancient history for being the victim of Sennacherib's invasion in 701 BCE. The Assyrians besieged Lachish with a large ramp, burned the city down, and led survivors away as captives. This event is hinted at in 2 Kings 18:13-16, in which Hezekiah sends a message to Sennacherib "at Lachish" asking for mercy and offering to pay a large tribute. Evidently Sennacherib's demonstration of his power at Lachish was enough to convince Hezekiah to end his resistance. The extent of Lachish's destruction is apparent in archaeological investigation of the site, which reveals a significant layer of ash and debris dating to this time period. The siege of Lachish is also depicted in a large stone relief that Sennacherib erected in his palace in Nineveh (and which is now in the British Museum). Shown in the relief are stout Assyrian soldiers attacking the city, killing defenders, and marching women and children into captivity.

This event is important in the history of Judah in that it cements their status as a vassal to the Assyrians for the next seventy-five years. The fact that Sennacherib finally spared the city of Jerusalem played a role in the development of Zion

Micah

theology. However, the destruction of Lachish may have negatively impacted Micah's perspective on the political and military leaders of Judah (cf. 1:13). Scholars have reasoned that Micah fled to Jerusalem in advance of the siege of Lachish. Whether or not this event precipitated his move to Jerusalem, Micah is highly critical of Judah's leaders and skeptical of their commitment to protect the people.

Many of Micah's oracles discuss the sins and punishment of both nations, Israel and Judah. Micah 1:6, for instance, says that God will "make Samaria a heap in the open country," which implies that Samaria has not yet been destroyed. In Micah 2:12, however, the prophet's prediction that God will "gather all of you, O Jacob" appears to address a nation already defeated and scattered. It has also been suggested that this text could date from the period of Judean exile after the destruction of Jerusalem in 586 BCE. Therefore, there is a wide range of possible historical backgrounds for individual oracles in the book. The reader must use care in identifying which audience and situation is the recipient of each oracle.

Micah includes references to two past historical periods as well. In 6:3-5 the prophet compares Judah's current situation to that of Israel during the exodus and wilderness wanderings. During that time, God delivered Israel from bondage in Egypt and protected them from the king of Moab, who commissioned Balaam to curse Israel. Now, the prophet says, they seek to return thanks to God with their ritual offerings rather than showing true service through acts of justice and mercy (6:6-8). The second mention of Israel's history is in Micah 6:16, which refers to the time of Ahab, the son of Omri. Ahab was king in the middle of the ninth century BCE and is described in 1 Kings 16–22 as a corrupt and greedy king. Micah says that the leaders of Israel have followed the legal practices and moral principles of Ahab's time and will therefore become a "horror" (NRSV "desolation") among their neighbors.

The final form of the book of Micah is most likely from the exilic period. Micah 4:9-10 presumes a future in which Judah has been defeated and exiled, without a king, to Babylon. The prophet promises that from Babylon, Judah shall be "rescued," that God will "redeem" them. In the time of Micah himself, such a specific reference to a Judean exile to Babylon would be unlikely. It is worth noting, however, that Isaiah responds to Hezekiah's overtures to the Babylonian king with a prediction of Babylonian exile (Isa 39:5-8). It may be that all references to Babylon found in the preexilic prophets are from later periods, but it is possible that Isaiah and Micah already anticipate the decisive role that Babylon would play in the downfall of Judah.

Theological Traditions

One emphasis that Micah shares with all preexilic prophets is his concern for economic injustice. In Micah 2:1-2 he describes business entrepreneurs who lie in their beds at night, plotting new schemes to cheat people out of homes and land. They have produced "wicked scales" and "dishonest weights" in order to enrich themselves deceitfully (6:11). Meanwhile, political leaders "abhor justice" (3:9-11), accept bribes, and permit the oppression of the poor. Micah compares the treatment of the poor to meat processing: the people are flayed, filleted, broken, and cooked "like meat in a kettle" (3:1-3). Even the prophets who should speak out against injustice have supported the delusions of the rich and powerful at the expense of the poor (3:5). Micah does mention other sins, such as religious idolatry (1:7; 5:12-14), but the main focus is on justice in the social and economic realms. Like Amos and Isaiah, Micah makes the point that God has no regard for the sacrificial offerings produced by people who do not fulfill the requirements of justice in their communal lives (6:6-8), the passage that contains the oft-quoted admonition that God prefers justice and mercy to ritual observance.

Micah expresses hope for the restoration of Israel and of Judah in times to come. Micah 2:12-13 describes a restored Israel as gathered sheep now nestled in a protective pasture. What is striking about this image is that no human king leads them: "Their king will pass on before them, the LORD at their head" (2:13b). It is possible that this text is an exilic addition since it seems to envision a post-monarchy world. However, it is not far removed from the classic statement of God's kingly rule on Mount Zion that Micah shares with Isaiah (4:1-3) or from other passages such as the claim that in days to come, "the LORD will reign over them in Mount Zion now and forevermore" (4:7b). Throughout the Zion tradition, the notion that the Davidic king is God's chosen ruler exists alongside the affirmation that God is the ultimate royal authority in Jerusalem. Micah says that even though God has executed justice against Israel and also threatened Judah with the same fate, the hope for both nations comes from what God will do through the Judean messiah (5:1-5). The king shall establish security and peace for both Judah and Israel only "in the strength of the LORD, in the majesty of the name of the LORD his God" (5:4).

One additional theological aspect of Micah is the *pathos* of the prophet, his feeling of pain and sorrow at the situation of his people. Micah's description of the violence and degradation of his people is highly emotional, and in two instances he expresses openly his emotional turmoil. Micah 1:8-9 proclaims the prophet's lament for the plight of Judah. Barefoot and naked (cf. Isa 20), he mourns for the troubles that have reached the gates of Jerusalem. Also striking is the prophet's call of despair in 7:1: "Woe is me!" He feels like a hungry person with nothing to satisfy his need for food, except here the prophet hungers for righteousness in a land overrun by injustice and violence. Now, he has become totally cynical about his own community. The "best" leaders are like "briers" (7:4), and people cannot even trust their friends or closest family members (7:5-6).

At the same time, Micah also feels a sense of fulfillment and even pride at the important task he has undertaken. The other prophets have failed in their duty to denounce injustice, but Micah feels empowered by "the spirit of the LORD" to pronounce God's judgment (3:8). The act of serving as God's prophet of judgment is an emotionally complex affair, a fact that will become clear in the story of Jeremiah.

Literary Features

The literary merits of Micah are not as obvious as the special features of Amos, Hosea, and Isaiah. The poetry of the book is emotionally powerful and tightly structured, and the prophet connects various images together in a creative way.

When reading through the book, notice the alternation between judgment and salvation oracles that continues through the whole book. Judgment oracles are found in 1:2–2:11, 3:1-12, 4:9–5:1, and 6:1–7:7 while salvation oracles alternate in 2:12-13, 4:1-8, 5:2-15, and 7:8-20. More than any other prophet book, Micah evenly balances the judgment of God with the hope for restoration. In the early part of the book, his rhetorical emphasis is on the message of judgment, while the salvation oracles tend to be shorter but with a compact punch. By the end, however, the promises of salvation have become the central theme, and even more astonishing is their radical universality. Micah suggests that Judah's restoration and forgiveness will be complete—and completely transformative for the world.

Another key literary feature of Micah is the use of direct address and quotation. Many of the oracles are directed in the second person, against "you." Micah begins by calling all of the earth's peoples to listen up (1:2), and the prophet singles out specific people for condemnation. For instance, he addresses "you" rulers (3:1), "you" prophets (3:6), and "you" rich people (6:13-16) who will be judged for caring more about their own comfort than justice. Micah also addresses Bethlehem directly (5:2), the city from whom will come the messiah, as well as the city of Jerusalem, who writhes in agony like a woman in labor (4:9-10).

The most common use of direct quotation is to provide the words of the wicked or misguided people who are about to be judged for their foolishness. The people tell the prophets, "Do not preach" (2:6), and honor the preacher who would say, "I will preach to you of wine and strong drink" (2:11). False prophets declare "peace" when they receive bribes but pronounce only contempt for those who will not pay them (3:5).

Rulers who have built their power by exploiting the people declare, "Surely the LORD is with us!" (3:11b). Micah 7:8-10 ends with a moving first-person glimpse into the pain and humiliation of Jerusalem, which has suffered for her sins: "Do not rejoice over me, O my enemy; when I fall, I shall rise." Through such direct quotation, the prophet is able not only to express the emotional content of the ideas but to switch quickly among the perspectives of different people. In 7:10a, for instance, Jerusalem's quotation is followed by one from the "enemy," saying, "Where is the LORD your God?" Through these quotations, the prophet evokes powerfully the different theological and emotional elements of a city's destruction.

Commentary

Micah 1–3

Micah begins with a series of visions directed against the northern kingdom of Israel and emphasizes that the lessons of Israel's fate reveal the need for Judah to remain true to God. In this, Micah shares much with the early chapters of Isaiah. Also, like the first five chapters of Isaiah, the final form of the book is complex and probably shows the work of a later editor in extending the prophecy to address Judah in exile, 150 years later.

The book of Micah shares many images and motifs with other prophetic books. It begins with a short description of the "day of the LORD," in which God marches forth as divine warrior (cf. Hab 3 and Zeph 1). He compares the idol worship of Samaria to the act of prostitution (1:7), an image we saw developed in great depth in Hosea. In vv. 8-9 the prophet laments and wails for the destruction of Israel and the threat to Judah. Such emotional reaction to God's judgment is a central feature of Jeremiah (cf. the "wound" of the people lamented by Jeremiah in 14:7–8), and the reference to Micah walking around naked brings to mind Isaiah's lengthy show of nakedness (Isa 20).

Chapters 2–3 focus on the corruption of Israel and Judah's political and religious leadership. Micah 2:1-5 describes real estate schemes by which poor people are defrauded of their homes and fields. God will punish these greedy landlords by parceling out their lands to invaders (2:5). Micah suggests that these privileged people are resistant to hearing his message, commanding him, "Do not preach . . . one should not preach of such things" (2:6). Like the self-deceptive worshipers that Jeremiah addresses in the temple (Jer 7:10), they are convinced that no harm can come to them. However, how can God let them continue to "rise up against my people as an enemy" (2:8)?

Micah 3:1-3 contains one of the most brutal metaphors for injustice in the prophets. He describes the leaders of Israel as cannibals who flay the people, cook their flesh and broken bones in a pot, and eat them. With biting sarcasm he then criticizes the prophets who "have something to eat" for declaring war against those who are hungry. Micah distances himself from these corrupt prophets (3:8) but predicts that God is about to bring an end to prophetic visions altogether (3:6-7). For more discussion of the cessation of prophecy as a divine judgment, see the discussion of Isaiah 28 in the previous chapter.

Chapter 3 ends by saying that the corruption seen among Israel's leadership extends as well to that of Judah. The rulers of Israel "abhor justice" while those of Judah "build Zion with blood" (3:10). Amos criticizes judges who take bribes (Amos 5:12; cf. Mic 7:3), but Micah goes further to say that priests only serve for money and prophets only give oracles for a fee (3:11). While they are corrupt, selfish, and rapacious, they are still (astonishingly) convinced of their own righteousness and believe that God will protect and bless them (3:11). It is because of these faithless and incompetent leaders that "Jerusalem shall become a heap of ruins" (3:12).

Micah

Micah 4–5

As pointed out above, Micah 4:1-3 is the same text as Isaiah 2:2-4. The additional verse in Micah 4:4 (which itself is similar to Zech 3:10, a postexilic text) suggests that the Isaiah text is the source for the one here. It may also be that the text originated somewhere else and made its way separately into these two books. Either way, the promise of restoration and exaltation of Jerusalem is a vivid and powerful vision. Notice the literary context in Micah: the prophet has just predicted that Jerusalem will become a heap of ruins and a forest on a hill; now he says that Jerusalem will be "established as the highest of the mountain," literally reversing the judgment in the previous oracle.

This oracle sets the stage for two chapters of salvation oracles, promising that God will heal and restore the exiled people of Israel (4:5-10; 5:7-9) and protect Judah from the invasion that is currently threatening her (4:11–5:1). This section is a meditation on the nature of strength and health. If the people "walk" in the name of God (4:5), then God will restore the "lame" and make them into a "strong nation" (4:7), leading to Jerusalem becoming again a "tower" with sovereignty (4:8). The armies that have camped against the city hope to violate and shame the city like a woman exposed (4:11; cf. Jerusalem as a woman in childbirth in 4:9-10). However, God's plan is to turn "daughter Zion" into a fierce animal with a sharp metal horn and hoofs. Notice that the prophet uses two images associated with weakness in the culture—those with a physical disability and women—and reverses the situation so that they become healthy and strong warriors. In some other places in the prophets, each of these is associated with moral weakness as well, but here the emphasis seems to be only on their physical vulnerability.

The catalyst for the salvation of Jerusalem will be the arrival of God's anointed king, who will establish the kingdom of Judah in strength and justice. Micah 5:2 is a key messianic text for Christian readers who connect the reference to Bethlehem to the birth story of Jesus (as in Matt 2:6). In this context, however, Micah describes a king who will rescue Judah from the Assyrian invasion. By mentioning the origins of David's family in Bethlehem, the prophet emphasizes the early history of the Davidic line rather than its largely disappointing succession of rulers in Jerusalem. Isaiah makes a similar move in referring to the messiah as the "stump of Jesse" (Isa 11:1).

Most astonishingly, the prophet suggests that when Assyria invades, Judah will defeat the Assyrian army with shepherds, who will establish themselves as kings and "rule the land of Assyria with the sword" (5:5-6). This will have the effect of freeing Israel from Assyrian bondage, which will empower them to become like a lion among animals, killing its enemies without opposition (5:8). Micah's prediction that God will have vengeance on the wicked, greedy nations who have invaded the lands of Israel and Judah is not unique in the prophets, but this is certainly the only place where we see Judah as the direct agent of that judgment.

Micah 6–7

Micah 6 is structured as a "covenant lawsuit," the *rib* that we saw in Hosea 4 and Isaiah 3 and that will figure prominently in Jeremiah. In Micah the jurors in the case that God brings against Israel are the creation itself, the mountains and the foundations of the earth (6:2). The next several verses present the substance of God's complaint against Israel, which is quite familiar from Amos and Hosea, though even more specific here: God brought Israel from Egypt through the exodus and protected them during the wilderness wanderings. In exchange for this unilateral salvation, God has told them what is expected of them: "to do justice, and to love kindness, and to walk humbly with your God" (6:8). Instead of offering true justice and righteousness, the people have tried to find God's favor through sacrifices and offerings.

The contrast between ritual worship and authentic service to God is found in several places in the prophets, such as Amos 5:21-24, Hosea 9:4, Isaiah 1:10-17, Isaiah 58:5-9, and others. In each of these texts, the people are performing normal, orthodox sacrificial rituals. These are not rites with syncretistic or polytheistic elements, yet God still rejects them wholesale. The reason is that all worship practices must be rooted in a fundamental commitment to justice that extends outside the sanctuary into the worlds of business, politics, courtrooms, and families. Each of the three items in Micah 6:8 is important. The leaders of Israel and Judah have been arrogant and grasping, forgetting that God is the source of their health and strength. If they are to walk (4:5-7), then they must walk in humility. We have discussed the meaning of *justice* in many places, but notice that the second item, translated "kindness" in the NRSV, is the key theological term *hesed*, better understood as "covenantal faithfulness." This term is one of the most theologically significant terms in the Hebrew Bible and appears often in connection with the Davidic covenant, where the NRSV usually translates it "steadfast love." With both translations, "kindness" and "steadfast love," it is essential to remember that the term does not refer to an emotional connection, a feeling of kindness or love. Rather, it is closer to loyalty, duty, and acts of faithfulness based on one's identity and prior commitments. If the people truly love *hesed*, then they will live in harmony with the requirements of the covenant naturally and gladly.

Micah 6:9–7:7 continues the description of Israel's depravity. In this section the prophet accuses them of using "dishonest weights," mentioned as well in Amos 8:5. The punishment of this economic injustice is that God will thwart their business plans: they will not be able to save any money, their agricultural products will not bear fruit, and they will "eat, but not be satisfied" (6:14-15). This last image is particularly important because it goes beyond famine to predict that the community will become dissatisfied and greedy in its corrupt business dealings and also in political, religious, and judicial matters. Micah 7:2b says that everyone hunts each other: "they all lie in wait for blood." Their princes and judges seek bribes and are like briers and thorns—sharp, injurious weeds that grab and hold others in their greed (7:4). This grasping corruption emerges even in family life, as parents and children treat each other with contempt and family members become enemies.

The book ends with three related oracles of salvation that most likely date to the exilic period. Micah 7:11-13 predicts the reestablishment of the national boundaries and the return of exiles from both Egypt and Assyria. Verse 14 says that this restoration will be accomplished by God, the "shepherd" of the people, who will lead and provide for them. When this happens, the nations that persecuted Israel will be humiliated and humbled and "come trembling out of their fortresses" to stand in fear of God (7:16-17). God will forgive the sins of Israel because of the divine commitment to the covenant with Israel, on behalf of Abraham and Jacob. God will show *hesed*, the "covenantal faithfulness" asked of the people in 6:8, by acting in ways that are true to the divine nature: "He does not retain anger forever, because he delights in showing clemency" (7:18b), an affirmation that resonates with the foundational description of God's character in Exodus 34:6-7.

Chapter 5

Zephaniah

Introduction

From a literary and theological point of view, Zephaniah is not as innovative as some of the other prophets, but he represents an important link between the four eighth-century BCE prophets and later prophetic books that inherit and reinterpret that tradition. Zephaniah's perspective is similar to that of First Isaiah, but his book addresses for the first time the changing situation of Judah in the latter half of the seventh century BCE. Although Zephaniah lived too early to perceive the major changes that were on their way at the end of the century, he played a role in keeping that tradition alive and active.

Historical Context

The history of Judah in the last half of the seventh century BCE is complex and, from a Judean perspective, disappointing. The Assyrian Empire had ruled the region for nearly a century but by 630 BCE had begun to lose its grip on western territories, including Egypt and Judah. In that year, according to 2 Kings 22–23, King Josiah instituted a series of sweeping religious reforms inspired by the rediscovery of the Mosaic Law book. He also extended political control not only over Judah but also within northern Israelite territory and westward toward the Mediterranean. Meanwhile, Egypt and Babylon formed an alliance against Assyria, and 2 Kings 23:23-30 states that Josiah attempted to oppose Egyptian expansion northward and was killed in battle by Pharaoh Neco in Megiddo. After this disaster, the fortunes of Judah declined rapidly. The Babylonians went on to usurp Assyrian power in the region and to force Judah into a vassal relationship. We will have more to say about the downfall of Assyria in our discussion of Nahum and about the disastrous last few years of Judah in the chapter on Jeremiah.

The prophecies of Zephaniah date to the period just before Josiah began his reforms. Although the book says that these oracles took place "in the days of King Josiah," there are no references in Zephaniah to Josianic reform, nor does the prophet express any hope for a resurgent Judean royal house. While the eighth-century BCE prophets reflect the beginning of Assyrian power in Judah and the early sixth-century BCE prophets witness the end of Judah as a nation, Zephaniah is a witness to the middle, to Judah as a nation independent yet under Assyrian domination. And yet the basic moral and social problems addressed by the prophet remain the same.

Theological Traditions

Similar to Isaiah and Micah, Zephaniah includes judgment oracles that affirm God's lordship over history and emphasize the covenantal requirements of justice and righteousness.

The aspect of Zephaniah's theology that has gained the most attention is his beautiful description of "the day of the LORD," a tradition that is mentioned in Amos 5:18-20 and is perhaps implied by a few references in Isaiah (e.g., Isa 2:17; 13:6-9). Zephaniah is the earliest known prophet to develop this metaphor fully, which in later times is employed by Jeremiah, Ezekiel, and Joel. In Zephaniah 1 the day of the Lord is described as the time when God will "make the wicked stumble (1:3), "punish the officials and the king's sons" (1:8), "punish the people who rest complacently" (1:12), and cause the blood of the wicked to be "poured out like dust" (1:17). According to 1:15 alone, the day of the Lord is a day of wrath, distress, anguish, ruin, devastation, darkness, gloom, and clouds. The next two chapters describe God's violent destruction of wicked enemies in Gaza, Moab, Nineveh, and so on. The hope of "that day," however, is that God will turn from judgment to mercy and gather other nations (3:8), as well as Judah (3:11), back to the Lord. On "that day" the Lord will be "in your midst" (3:15, 17), which will bring an end to fear, disaster, and oppression for God's people.

Literary Features

For a short book, Zephaniah covers a wide range of prophetic expression. Zephaniah begins with an image of God's judgment on the day of the Lord (ch. 1), pronounces God's judgment on foreign nations (ch. 2), and balances the judgment of Israel with hope for future restoration (ch. 3). The rhetorical shifts from the beginning of the book to its end are striking. Notice the total destruction predicted in 1:2, in which God says, "I will utterly sweep away everything from the face of the earth." The rest of chapter 1 describes in detail the "full" and "terrible end" that God is bringing upon the earth. However, in chapter 2 we find references to a faithful remnant that may survive the judgment (2:3) and to God's people who will benefit from the destruction of their enemies (2:7, 9). Finally, in the salvation oracle in chapter 3, God declares that the divine plan is to redeem all the world's peoples (3:9) and establish Judah among the nations with renown and praise (3:20).

In the context of the whole book, therefore, the vision of total destruction in chapter 1 is purely rhetorical. The prophet's point is not that God is going to utterly destroy everything, even though that is what he says. Rather, this first section establishes the profound justice of God's judgment. It is within God's right to utterly unmake creation itself, and so when God's larger purpose of salvation and world peace emerges, it reveals the goodness and mercy of God even more powerfully.

Commentary

Zephaniah 1–3

Zephaniah begins with a rousing judgment oracle against the whole creation, with God saying, "I will utterly sweep away everything," including humans, animals, birds, and fish. The reason for this harsh judgment is that the people have worshiped other gods, namely Baal (1:4), the "host of heaven" (i.e., astral deities), and Milcom (i.e., Molech, 1:5). Other prophets have said that human sin and God's judgment will have negative effects on the natural world (e.g., Isa 34:13; Jer 9:11), but this is the most extreme expression of this idea. The judgment described by Zephaniah is even more complete than the Genesis flood, since even the fish are destroyed in God's "sweeping away." The severity of this punishment echoes Amos, and the prophet uses the language of Hosea to describe Judah's sin as "turning back" from following God (1:6). The covenant they have shared is now broken by their faithless worship of other gods. This is the same situation that lies behind Amos's declaration that "the end" has come upon Israel (Amos 8:3) and Hosea's statement that Israel is "not my people" (Hos 1:9).

The next image is even more striking, if somewhat obscure. God has prepared a sacrifice and consecrated those who have been invited (1:7). The irony is that these guests are to serve as the actual sacrificial offerings. The prophet, therefore, has borrowed the language of the sacrificial cult to describe God's judgment on wicked people, which shockingly turns the ritual into a kind of human sacrifice. This image is surprisingly common in the prophets (see Isa 30:27-33; 34:6; Jer 46:10; Ezek 39:17-20). In each of these, God kills wicked people as part of a sacrificial offering, and in the Ezekiel passage these victims even become food for the righteous. This language, however, is metaphorical. The image is meant to convey God's righteous judgment and not to say anything about human sacrifice.

In v. 7 Zephaniah mentions "the day of the Lord," the time when God will come as judge, king, and warrior to bring judgment on the divine enemies. We discussed this idea already in reference to Amos 5:18-20, but Zephaniah develops the image in much more detail. He says that the day of the Lord is a time of divine violence, in which God "will search Jerusalem with lamps" in order to punish the people. They have been resting complacently, expecting that God will do nothing, neither "good" nor "harm" (1:12). Paraphrasing Amos 5:11, Zephaniah says that these indolent people will construct houses and vineyards but will not live to benefit from them (1:13). The money that they have accumulated will not be able to rescue them from their distress (1:18). The ruin, devastation, and anguish of that day will be complete and universal, bringing a "full, terrible end" to all of the earth's people.

The one slight text of hope in Amos (prior to the salvation oracles in 9:11-15) suggests that people may "seek the LORD and live" (Amos 5:4), but Amos goes on to say that God will personally pursue and destroy all survivors of the coming collapse (Amos 9). A similar tension operates in Zephaniah; after promising a "full, terrible end," he suggests that if people "seek the LORD" in righteousness and humility, then they may survive the day of the Lord (2:3). As chapter 2 continues, we realize that the universal destruction predicted in chapter 1 is a rhetorical overstatement. God will bring judgment on the city-states and nations of Gaza, Phoenicia, Moab, Ammon, Ethiopia, and Assyria, but the result of this will be relief and restoration for the Judeans who have been persecuted by them (2:7, 9; 3:19-20).

Even though the day of the Lord begins with heavy of judgment for Judah and Jerusalem, quickly the focus changes so that the time of God's wrath will be good news for God's people, at least for the "humble of the land" (2:3). The theme of desolation that began the book is applied consistently to the foreign nations who will suffer on the day of the Lord. Gaza will be deserted (2:4); Philistia will be depopulated (2:5); Moab will become a wasteland like Sodom and Gomorrah (2:9); and Nineveh will be "a desolation, a dry waste like the desert" (2:13) and "a lair for wild animals" (2:15). Zephaniah anticipates the gleeful taunt over a despoiled Nineveh that we find in Nahum. The difference is that Zephaniah is written while Nineveh is still very much an international force. Its fall from power was swift and total, which helps explain Nahum's elated glee.

Zephaniah 3 turns the prophet's gaze back to Judah, describing Zion as a "soiled, defiled, oppressing city" (3:1). Like Micah, the prophet places most of the blame on the city's leadership. The people have "listened to no voice" and "not trusted in the LORD" (3:2), primarily because the political leaders are predatory, the prophets are faithless, and the priests are profane (3:3-4), the exact opposite of how they are supposed to be in order to perform their duties properly. Princes and judges are supposed to protect the weak, not prey on them, and religious leaders are supposed to fight against doubt, apathy, and abominations, not promote them.

God says that previous warnings have failed to grab the city's attention, so nations are being assembled to bring a purifying force of divine judgment on them (3:7-8). The result of this process will be the removal of the high and mighty, powerful and arrogant, leaving only the humble, righteous, and honest remnant (3:11-13). As in Micah 2:13 the restored community is gathered around the Lord as king; there is no human king mentioned in 3:14-20. Instead of kings who fail to execute justice and righteousness, now God is "in your midst," says the prophet, and God will be the one to protect them from enemies (3:15), support the weak and vulnerable (3:19), and establish the people among the nations (3:20). These are traditional roles of a king, and with the utter failure of Judah's royal leadership, God will be the only king they need.

Chapter 6

Nahum

Introduction

The book of Nahum has two dominant characteristics. First, it is a literary masterpiece, composed of breathless and breathtaking poetry. Second, its subject matter and theology appear to many readers as gruesome, barbaric, and offensive. It is the kind of biblical text that is too interesting to ignore completely but that causes a certain discomfort when seen as part of the Christian or Jewish canon. In reading this book we will focus on the powerful poetic imagery and language in Nahum and consider the theological contribution of the book within the canon. Theologically, the issue is what our *stance* should be toward the book: Can readers find positive and enriching theology in the book, or should they *stand against* the book, opposing its perspective and objecting to its brutality?

We should not overstate the issue. Nahum is not more violent or theologically troubling than some stories in Joshua and Judges, and it draws upon images of God that are found as well in Psalms, Isaiah, and Job. The main obstacle for modern readers of Nahum is that it focuses almost exclusively on the theme of God's wrath, whereas the other prophets include uplifting passages that dilute the negativity of the violent passages. As a result the book as a whole is sometimes passed over as readers quickly turn to other books that may seem more in harmony with their own theology. Our task in this chapter is to understand the way in which Nahum draws upon poetic imagery and to show why he develops his prophetic insights in such a manner. After interpreting the oracles themselves, we are better able to consider how Nahum's insights might encourage, challenge, or distress us in our own context.

Historical Context

The prophet Nahum delivered these oracles during the last half of the seventh century BCE in Judah. This period was one of great upheaval in the ancient Near Eastern world. As seen in the discussion of Amos and Hosea, Assyria had turned its imperial might toward the west in the last half of the eighth century. They conquered the northern kingdom of Israel after a three-year siege of Samaria, concluded in 722 BCE. Except for a few rebellious moments, the kings of Judah responded by bowing to the Assyrians, becoming vassals of the great empire. However, after the death of the last Assyrian king, Ashurbanipal, in 630, Assyrian power quickly dissipated. The Judean king Josiah benefited from this development by sponsoring an independence movement and religious reform around the year 620 (2 Kgs 22–23). The power vacuum left by the weakened Assyrians was soon filled, however, by the ascendant neo-Babylonian Empire under the leadership of Nabopolassar. By the end of the seventh century, Judah had transferred its allegiance to the Babylonians.

The superscription to the book of Nahum makes reference to Nineveh, the Assyrian capital city that fell to the Babylonians in 612. Since the oracles seem to predict this destruction rather than describe it, they should be dated earlier than 612 but later than the fall of Thebes in 663, an event mentioned in Nahum 3:8. The downfall of the Assyrian capital is presented as a message of hope and deliverance to the people of Judah, which supports the argument that these oracles originated before the Assyrians had lost their hold on Judah. By the time Nineveh was destroyed, Assyria would not have been understood to be as big of a threat as the Egyptians and Babylonians. It is possible, however, that the oracles were delivered as late as 612 BCE, since the memory of Assyria's greatness would have still been strong.

Theological Traditions

Two basic theological ideas undergird the book of Nahum. First is the conviction that God has the power to direct world affairs, and second is that God uses that power to execute justice against every nation in the world, Judah and beyond.

God as Lord of History

In the ancient Near East, there were various levels of authority in the divine world: "High gods" rule over nature, patron deities sponsor particular cities or tribes, and personal deities work on behalf of particular individuals. God is considered the patron deity of the Israelites (see Deut 32:8-9), and each of the surrounding nations has one or more deities of its own. When two armies collide, the natural conclusion is that the god of the victorious army has defeated the god of the vanquished one. Often, the Assyrians would carry the statues of conquered deities home with them into "exile" to symbolize this divine victory. This idea underpins the speech of the Assyrian official to the residents of Jerusalem in Isaiah 36:18-20: "Has any of the gods of the nations saved their land out of the hand of the king of Assyria? Where are the gods of Hamath and Arpad? Where are the gods of Sepharvaim? Have they delivered Samaria out of my hand? Who among all the gods of these countries have saved their countries out of my hand, that the LORD should save Jerusalem out of my hand?"

In the oracles against the nations, the prophets declare that God has the power to destroy foreign evildoers. The most remarkable aspect, however, is that God's show of power has nothing to do with Israel's or Judah's military might. Rather, these oracles claim that God directs the military might of another conquering nation, specifically the Assyrians,

Babylonians, or Egyptians. Jeremiah 47, for example, contains an oracle celebrating the impending doom of the Philistines at the hand of Nebuchadnezzar in 604. Verse 4 says that "the LORD is destroying the Philistines." Jeremiah 48 continues with an oracle against Moab, Israel's old enemy from the eastern bank of the Jordan River. Verse 7 declares that "Chemosh [the Moabite deity] shall go out into exile, with his priests and his attendants." From the perspective of the Babylonians and their victims, these events have nothing to do with Judah or its deity. The prophets, however, present a completely different view of world history, in which geopolitical events have their source and significance in the will of God.

Divine Justice

This leads to the second theological notion behind these oracles. God directs sovereign power over world affairs with a single purpose: to avenge wicked behavior. In our discussion of Amos 1–2, we saw that God's acts of judgment are in response to particular atrocities and injustices. A central affirmation in the biblical tradition is that God richly rewards obedience with blessing and reluctantly punishes disobedience (see Lev 26 and Deut 28). In this case, however, the punishment of foreign nations has nothing to do with their regard or disregard for God nor with their fulfillment of God's laws. Rather, the complaint is based on universal virtues such as respect for life, care for the weak and needy, moderation, and humility. These oracles are filled with indictments of foreign nations who have swallowed up other nations, killed people cruelly, and scattered them throughout the earth, all the while boasting arrogantly of their power, even their divinity (see Ezek 28:2). The most common victim of the wicked acts mentioned in these prophecies is Israel or Judah, but this is not always the case. God punishes arrogant and violent nations not merely for attacking his chosen people but for acting in a way that puts any innocent nation in peril.

The oracles against the nations reveal God's vengeance against wicked kings and nations everywhere. God has the power to carry out this agenda and acts only with proper cause, that is, the righting of grievous wrongs. The term "vengeance" often has a negative connotation, perhaps because it is increasingly associated with individual "vigilante" justice outside of the proper authorities. In the ancient world, however, there were no international courts to hold nations accountable for their greedy and sadistic acts. It is understandable that a small nation like Judah would look to their God to institute justice. God takes up that responsibility most dramatically in Psalm 82, in which the other world deities are condemned for their refusal to judge the earth rightly. The prophets indicate that God can use world powers against each other to achieve this purpose. Shortly after Nahum, Habakkuk questions God's choice of instrument, the Babylonians, arguing that the cure may be worse than the illness.

Literary Features

Oracles Against the Nations

Nahum's oracles are part of a widespread prophetic tradition, that of the so-called "oracles against the nations." Such texts may be found as well in Amos 1–2, Isaiah 13–23, Zephaniah 2–3, Jeremiah 46–51, Obadiah, and Ezekiel 25–32. The important thing to remember about these oracles is that although they denounce the evils of other nations and declare God's intention to bring judgment, they are delivered to Israelite or Judean audiences. Thus, the standard distinction between a "judgment oracle" and a "salvation oracle" becomes blurred. The words of judgment against these nations serve as a comforting word of salvation to the Israelites and Judeans who suffer at foreign hands. The nations being judged would not have heard these oracles, so the announcement of their judgment is a message of salvation to the actual audience. For more on this literary type, see the discussion of the texts cited previously.

Imagery

The primary image of God in the book of Nahum is one of anger and might. In chapter 1 the prophet draws upon creation imagery to demonstrate God's fearsome power (Nah 1:4-5), which we see also in Habakkuk and Isaiah. The creation of the cosmos is pictured as a great battle between God and the power of chaos, symbolized by the primordial waters that survive in the form of seas and rivers. For other examples of this creation motif, see Psalm 74:12-17; 89:5-14; Job 38; and Habakkuk 3.

The most memorable sections of Nahum are the visions of battle in 2:3-9 and 3:1-7. The people being addressed by the prophet are the inhabitants and rulers of Nineveh, but the real audience is the prophet's community in Judah. Presumably they have heard about the fall of the great Assyrian city, though this might be their first exposure to the news. In the age before newspapers, satellite television, and the Internet, how did people learn about and contextualize foreign events? In this text the prophet describes what has happened in imaginative detail. The purpose, of course, is to gloat over the fall of their enemy, but the effect of the prophet's poetry is to make that faraway event real in their minds.

This is certainly a text that would benefit from being read in a variety of translations, as there are different ways of handling this intense imagery. The prophet describes the color of the uniforms, the glint of metal in the sunlight, the sounds of shouting from both victorious and defeated sides, and the final chaotic tumble of those who are dead, fleeing, and pursuing.

Nahum also uses a misogynistic image in 3:4-7, similar to those found in Hosea 1–3, Jeremiah 13:20-27, and Ezekiel 16 and 23. In these passages the prophet compares the guilty and punished people to sexually corrupt women who are publicly shamed and attacked. The image of "lifting your skirts over your face" implies shame and degradation and is rooted in a problematic image of women as the property of their father or husband, and whose sexuality is a moral weakness that must be carefully controlled. For more on this, see the chapter on Hosea.

Commentary

Nahum 1–2

Nahum wastes no time getting to the point of his book: "A jealous and avenging God is the LORD; the LORD is avenging and wrathful" (1:2). The two most important descriptive terms here are "jealous" and "avenging." The jealousy of God is an expression of divine uniqueness, power, and worthiness. The concept appears most often within threats of punishment for not obeying God's Law (Ex 20:5; 34:4; Deut 4:24). Thus, God does not avenge out of passion or irrational emotion; God is "slow to anger" (Exod 34:6-7) but resolute when provoked.

From the beginning of Nahum, the readers confront basic questions of fairness and compassion, of God's mercy and wrath. In commenting on this passage, J. J. M. Roberts writes, "One should beware of any bogus morality that dismisses vengeance as both inappropriate to humans and unworthy of God. Such a view simply betrays a glaring absence of the most elementary sense of justice." In other words, as we read this book, we should consider that God serves as prosecutor, judge, and executioner in a kind of international criminal court. The Assyrians, of course, would not consider God to have the power or authority to assume such an exalted place. This oracle, however, is not delivered to the Assyrians, but to the Judeans, who are coming to view God as the judge of all the earth (Gen 18:25).

Nahum 3

Chapter 3 begins with a genre known traditionally as a "woe oracle." The King James Version begins with "Woe to the bloody city!" and the New International Version reads, "Woe to the city of blood." The Hebrew term translated "woe" is *hoy*, which means something closer to "Hey, you!" and can be seen in the New Revised Standard Version's translation, "Ah! City of bloodshed." The term is used in funeral songs in which the deceased person was addressed directly, as in David's lament over Absalom (2 Sam 18:33), and appears in Isaiah 55:1 with no hint of the concept of woe: "*Hoy* all who thirst, come to the waters." The term indicates, therefore, that the oracle is addressed directly to the city and calls for the city's attention with the exclamation "Hey, you!"

This oracle describes the coming destruction of the city by a fierce army, already seen in the oracle to the Assyrian king in chapter 2. They are fast and vigorous, overrunning the city and killing its inhabitants: "Horsemen charging, flashing sword and glittering spear, piles of dead, heaps of corpses, dead bodies without end—they stumble over the bodies" (3:3). The dramatic language is colorful and terse, evoking scenes of destruction with a minimum of words. The first several verses consist almost entirely of nouns and participles, the "-ing" verbal form that emphasizes immediate and ongoing action. The prophet is not simply conveying information about future events but drawing his audience into the scene by capturing their imaginations. Although the oracle addresses the city, it is designed to affect its real audience, the people of Judah.

This scene of destruction leads directly to a passage of indictment, giving the legal justification for this violent punishment. Echoing passages in Hosea, Jeremiah, and Ezekiel, the wicked city of Nineveh is presented as a harlot, a "gracefully alluring mistress of sorcery" (3:4). Like the "strange woman" of Proverbs 7, the harlot has enticed her victims with seductive charm, looking to snare them in a trap. Because she has used her beautiful body to bring others to harm, the punishment is that her naked body shall be exposed to the public, and she shall be reviled and rejected (cf. Isa 47:1-3). For more on the use of feminine imagery to evoke shock and dismay, see our previous discussion of Hosea. It suffices to say here that the image of a beautiful woman humiliated in public served the prophet's rhetorical intention: to get the audience's attention and to evoke a certain image of God's righteous anger. In their hierarchical and sometimes misogynistic culture, the men in the audience would have known how to treat a wayward wife or daughter and would have identified with God, the male authority doling out just punishment. Significantly, when this metaphor is used elsewhere in the prophets, the (mostly male) audience is compared to the *woman* rather than to the righteous man, which would have been shocking and disorienting.

The image of humiliation continues with an analogy to Thebes, the great Egyptian city conquered by the Assyrians in 663. Thebes is pictured as a noble city protected by natural defenses (a watery moat) and strong benefactors (the northern African nations of Ethiopia, Egypt, Put, and Libya), which nevertheless is captured and taken into exile. As a consequence the city's children are dashed upon the paved street, and its leaders are carried into exile. Like that great city taken by the Assyrians, the Assyrian capital of Nineveh will be captured, its defenses like ripe figs falling into eager mouths. Like a woman with her skirts over her head, the city's gate stands open and unprotected.

The prophet taunts the city by challenging it to prepare defenses, multiply its economic and military prowess, and prepare for a siege. Such strength will be of no use, however, because the city inhabitants will be killed within their fortifications, and their defenders will disappear like a swarm of locusts that quickly vanishes. He finishes with a final metaphor, the city as a herd of sheep without a shepherd, wandering without protection on the mountainside. The image of leaders as shepherds is quite common in the prophetic literature (see Jer 23 and Ezek 34). Each image in this chapter expresses the same basic point—that the city is vulnerable and without help. Former lovers and protectors, stout defenses, swarms of guards, city leaders—none of these will prove of any benefit when the attack comes. "There is no assuaging your hurt, your wound is mortal," the prophet proclaims (3:19). The peoples who have suffered under the brutal rule of Assyria will only clap and rejoice when the city is destroyed with a taste of its own cruel medicine.

Chapter 7

Habakkuk

Introduction

From the first two verses of Habakkuk, readers are aware that this is an unusual book, despite the fairly normal-sounding introduction. It begins with a standard formulation: "The oracle that the prophet Habakkuk saw" (Habakkuk is the earliest prophet who receives the specific designation "the prophet"). Verse 2, though, does not sound like "prophecy" at all: "O Lord, how long shall I cry for help, and you will not listen?"

Readers may wonder if the Bible has somehow turned back a few hundred pages to the Psalms, for a "lament psalm" begins this book of prophecy. After this unusual beginning, Habakkuk includes a dialogical dispute similar to the one in Job, as well as a remarkable praise hymn of "theophany." Along the way Habakkuk develops some of the most sensitive theological reflection in the prophets and encourages his listeners and readers to remain faithful and patient even when there is no evidence of God's good providence in the world around them.

Habakkuk has an odd-sounding name to English readers, which may account for some of its relative obscurity. This short prophetic book, however, is a treasure that will greatly reward one's close study.

God's Servants, the Prophets

Historical Context

After the Assyrian invasion that began during the time of Isaiah (730s–700 BCE), a long period of relative calm had settled in Judah, anchored by the fifty-five-year reign of Manasseh in the first half of the seventh century. With the decline of Assyrian power and the fall of Nineveh in 612 BCE (celebrated so gleefully by Nahum), chaos once again engulfed the region. As Assyria crumbled, there was initially some hope that Judah might stand again on her own without foreign interference. This window of opportunity led to the religious reforms and political resurgence of Josiah in the 630s and 620s BCE (see 2 Kgs 22–23). Josiah's hopes were dashed, however, when the Assyrian Empire was replaced by the neo-Babylonian Empire. Nebuchadnezzar defeated the Egyptians and Assyrians at Carchemish in 605 BCE and became the major power in the biblical world. Judah bec-206ame a vassal of the Babylonians, and within two decades the nation was dismantled and its people exiled.

Habakkuk was written near the beginning of this terrible time for Judah. The reference to the Chaldean army in 1:6 implies that the Babylonian army under Nebuchadnezzar is in the early stages of its conquest. Jehoiakim, king of Judah (608–598 BCE), had been placed on the throne by the Egyptian pharaoh Neco, replacing his brother Jehoahaz three months after the death of their father, Josiah, in 609 BCE. Jehoiakim served as a vassal of the Egyptians until Nebuchadnezzar defeated them soundly at Carchemish in 605 BCE, at which time Jehoiakim switched his allegiance to the Babylonians. After some time Jehoiakim evidently came to believe that Nebuchadnezzar could not project real power southward into the Levant, so the Judean king withheld tribute and rebelled against the Babylonians. Jehoiakim miscalculated badly; Nebuchadezzar invaded Judah in 598–597, and Jehoiakim died during the siege, replaced by his son Jehoiachin. A more extended discussion of this historical period in Judah can be found in the chapter on Jeremiah.

Other than Habakkuk's mention of the Chaldean army, the only other historical reference in the book is to the presence of injustice and lack of legal enforcement: "So the law becomes slack and justice never prevails. The wicked surround the righteous—therefore judgment comes forth perverted" (1:4). Such a situation is not unique to this time period. However, this complaint does make more sense prior to the exile when there is still a legally established government charged with executing justice and protecting the weak. The situation is similar to that of Amos, Hosea, and Isaiah. Habakkuk, despite his literary uniqueness, fits firmly within the larger preexilic prophetic tradition. This preexilic period is nearing its end, however, and Habakkuk has already begun reflecting on the theological and human consequences of God's judgment on sinful Judah.

Theological Traditions

Many of the theological themes we have seen in earlier books apply here as well, especially the decisive link between righteousness and economic justice. Habakkuk presumes a covenantal relationship between God and the people but does not refer specifically to any parts of the tradition.

Theodicy

Habakkuk is singular in his engagement with the theodicy and lament traditions. "Theodicy" refers to the problem of innocent suffering in the world: If God is powerful and loving, how can the righteous suffer? And given that we do see unjust suffering in the world, how can we affirm the justice of God? In the lament psalms we see individuals and the community struggle to understand why illness, disease, or calamity have fallen upon them. It may be the result of a deserved divine punishment (e.g., Ps 51) or simply the work of wicked people (e.g., Ps 22). Either way, the psalmist trusts in the power of God to save and to heal and calls on God to rise up and have mercy upon those who suffer.

Consider as well the book of Job, which contains one of the most complex and sustained reflections on innocent suffering in the ancient world. Job's conversations with God and with his "friends" is similar to Habakkuk's questioning of God in the first two chapters. Job's complaints grow out of his own sufferings, from which he extrapolates to criticize God's governance of the wider world. Habakkuk, on the other hand, looks across the horizon and wonders at what he sees. How could God fulfill divine purposes by using a foreign invasion that will bring death and pestilence in its wake? Why would God use a wicked nation bent only on increasing its wealth and power? By connecting to the prophetic idea of "dual agency" (cf. Isa 10:5-19), Habakkuk affirms in the end that God's purposes will transcend the smaller events that work together to fulfill them. In the face of such a vast mystery, the prophet counsels patient waiting as well as the empathetic recognition of unjust suffering.

Theophany

One area where Habakkuk breaks new ground is in his use of theophany in chapter 3, a motif that we discussed in relation to Isaiah 6 and Nahum. The word *theophany* means the appearance of God in a particular time and place, and "theophanic" visions often include standard features such as earthquake, lightning, and thunder. In the face of power, the one witnessing the theophany has a physical reaction of fear and trembling. In many theophany passages God appears to someone in order to deliver a message or to commission a prophet to fulfill a certain task, such as the call of Isaiah to preach and of Moses to liberate his people. In Habakkuk the theophany reassures the prophet that God is active in the world, has power over all natural and human forces in the creation, and will save the people from their enemies. Whereas Habakkuk begins with a question about "how long" God will remain indifferent to the cries of the oppressed, it ends with a vivid demonstration of God's sovereignty and agency in the world.

Habakkuk

Literary Features

Habakkuk is a literary masterpiece. It is not as long or as complex as Isaiah or as dramatically creative as Hosea, but it is tightly constructed, vivid in its imagery, and inventive in the way it draws upon a variety of literary genres and motifs. As always, the poetry demands to be read slowly and with repetition. In a class context this would be an excellent book for participants to dramatize, perhaps by first rewriting the text in their own words.

Dialogue

We have seen in a few passages that it is important to pay attention to the speaker and audience of particular verses. At times it is not immediately obvious that a change in speaker has occurred, which could lead to an odd misinterpretation of a passage. In Habakkuk the alternation between speakers (in this case God and Habakkuk) is regular but not always well marked. Habakkuk and God exchange two rounds of question and answer in 1:2–2:3. After Habakkuk's questioning of God in 1:2-4, God begins to respond in v. 5, though there is no narrative transition in the text. Notice the parallels between the question and answer: the prophet says that God makes him "see wrongdoing," and God tells him to "look at the nations, and see!" God answers his question by redirecting his gaze.

Habakkuk's voice is again heard as the prophet responds by saying that God's "eyes are too pure to behold evil" but that God has seen suffering and is "silent" (1:13). Habakkuk then promises to "keep watch," to which God responds that he should "write the vision" in such large letters that even a person running by could read it (2:2), the ancient equivalent of a billboard.

Woe Oracles

The series of five oracles in 2:6-19 follow a standard prophetic genre known as the "woe oracle," which we saw also in

Nahum. The Hebrew term *hoy* means "Hey, you!" or "Ah!" and is sometimes spoken about a person and sometimes directly addressed to the individual in question. The direct address "Alas to you!" or "Ah! You!" is the formula here, and the whole section is constructed as a second-person address. The speaker may be Habakkuk interpreting the vision he has seen, but most likely these doomed people are being addressed by the divine voice itself. See the section on chapters 1–2 for discussion of the biting irony in these oracles and Nahum 3 for further discussion of *hoy* oracles.

Praise Hymns

The majestic poem in chapter 3 contains a theophanic vision. As a whole, however, it takes the form of a praise hymn with two rhetorical purposes: to ask God for help and to provide reassurance that God has the power to fulfill the divine promises. It has been common in biblical scholarship to divide psalms into two basic modes: petition or praise. More recently, however, interpreters have paid more attention to the interconnections between these two modes, both in terms of literary form and rhetorical context. Consider, for example, Psalm 33, a praise hymn that includes similar creation or cosmic imagery found in Habakkuk 3. Psalm 33:7 says that God has "gathered the waters of the sea as in a bottle," an allusion to God's victory over chaos at creation, as in Habakkuk 3:8, 10, and 15. Also, notice how Psalm 33, like Habakkuk, connects this power over creation to God's power over human rulers and armies (33:13-17) and ends with a call for the persecuted to remain faithful and wait patiently for the Lord's deliverance (33:20-22). Some scholars have argued that these last three verses were added later as the "praise" hymn was repurposed as part of a later "petition." At least in the current form, however, there are profound connections between those literary and rhetorical modes. The offering of praise may motivate God to act in ways that are consistent with such a sterling description and may give worshipers a new mental and spiritual context in which to endure their suffering.

Commentary

Habakkuk 1–2

Habakkuk 1–2 takes the form of a dialogue between God and the prophet. Habakkuk speaks in 1:2-4 and 1:12–2:2, and God answers in 1:5-11 and 2:2-3. The remainder of chapter 2 is a complex vision report that God tells Habakkuk to "write" down and is a meditation on the transcendence of the Lord's plans over prideful human desires and intentions.

As discussed in the introductory paragraphs, Habakkuk begins with a lament psalm in which he complains that God has not responded either to his cries for help or to the plain fact of injustice and wickedness that runs rampant in the community. Compare this lament language to that in Psalm 74:10: "How long, O God, is the foe to scoff? Is the enemy to revile your name forever?" (see also Pss 13:1; 35:17; 94:3; Job 19:2). The only other time the "How long?" formula is used in the prophets is in Zechariah 1:12, in which an angel intercedes with God to have mercy and forgive Jerusalem. These lament psalms generally arise from personal trials and sufferings of the psalmist. Habakkuk is different in that he does not say that he himself is the victim of injustice. Rather, he borrows the lament formula in order to proclaim his prophetic message against the injustice in his nation, which has the effect of putting the blame, to some degree, on God's inaction.

God responds to the prophet and promises that things are about to change: "For a work is being done in your days that you would not believe if you were told" (1:5b). God is "rousing" the Chaldeans and sending them against kings and nations. God's speech reflects awe at the strength and fearsomeness of the Babylonian army and implies that they are the answer to the prophet's question: "Their justice and dignity proceed from themselves" (1:7b).

The prophet cannot imagine how such a violent enemy could be the agent and deliverer of God's justice. In 1:12-17 he makes two observations: first that God is righteous and second that the Babylonians are enemies that kill their victims and worship their weapons (1:16). How can a holy God be involved with such as these? This is the only direct challenge to the justice of God in the prophets. By contrast, Jeremiah complains about God's use of him, but his complaint isn't about God's use of violent armies; rather, it is about his delay in sending that army (Jer 20:7-10). Habakkuk finishes with the determination to stand at his "watchpost" and keep looking for God's answer to his question.

The answer comes in the form of a vision that predicts eventual retribution on all who are greedy and rapacious, which presumably includes both the wicked people in Judah as well as the Chaldean army. The righteous are promised life if they remain faithful: "the righteous live by their faith," a verse quoted three times in the New Testament (2:4; Rom 1:7; Gal 3:11; Heb 10:38). This hopeful promise may seem hollow in a world so filled with violence. God says, however, that the time of deliverance is "appointed" and will not turn out false, encouraging the people that "if it seems to tarry, wait for it" (2:3b). As the prophetic tradition develops into apocalypticism, this emphasis on appointed times and patient waiting becomes even more central.

Verse 5 compares the wicked people in the world to "Sheol," the grave that finally envelops all living things, and to "Death," which is never satiated. "Death" here may be a reference to the Canaanite deity Mot, who is pictured in mythology as a giant mouth with one lip to the heavens and one lip to earth, swallowing up everything in his path. Even enemies like this will fall into ruin.

The idea is that God's actions are complex and reveal themselves over the long term, but one may be sure of God's fundamental commitment to justice and righteousness. This passage resonates with Isaiah's statement that God is using the Assyrian army as a tool of judgment and will next turn to punishing the Assyrians for their greedy violence (Isa 10:5-19). Here again we see the idea of "dual agency" at work. The foreign king has his own agency (decisions and purposes) while God uses the king's actions for the divine agency. The king does not need to know that he is being used, or even be "worthy" of such use, for God's purposes to be fulfilled.

Habakkuk 2:6-20 contains a series of five "woe oracles," or expressions of doom for guilty people, and is a breathtaking expression of prophetic contempt for economic and social injustice. The prophet denounces people who get rich through unfair financial deals (2:6-8), use that money to build beautiful houses on the mountain (2:9-11), develop real estate with exploited labor (2:12-14), promote vice and addiction in order to enjoy the dissolution of their neighbors (2:15-17), and reject true worship of God for the veneration of idols (2:18-19). Each of these woe oracles uses the rhetorical technique of irony. For example, those who have gotten rich by loaning money will find themselves as plunder for their creditors. Those who build fine homes will see that the stone and wood of their houses has turned against them, and those who force other people to get drunk will have "the cup in the LORD's right hand" forced upon them, leading to contempt, shame, and destruction (2:16). When these guilty people turn for help to the idols they have made, they will discover that these silent objects have no power at all.

Although the world may seem chaotic and out of control, God is present in the temple in Jerusalem (2:20). Although the wicked, greedy, and violent people in this world may think they have liberty to act however they wish for their own pleasure, they will soon discover that God will not let such injustice go unpunished. In the face of this holy and just God, the prophet says, "Let all the earth keep silence before him" (2:20).

Habakkuk 3

Habakkuk 3 is a praise hymn in which the prophet celebrates God's powerful work in the world. It may have been added to the first two chapters by a later hand, but either way it certainly works well as the conclusion to the vision of God's justice in chapter 2. Like many praise hymns, the poem celebrates what has been done *in the past* with an implicit call for

GOD'S SERVANTS, THE PROPHETS

God to rise up and do similarly amazing things *now*. Verse 2 says that the poet stands "in awe" of God's work and asks God to "in our own time revive it; in our own time make it known."

The theophany that follows uses natural imagery to show God as the mighty divine warrior. The Lord's power radiates visibly and palpably, devastating all forces natural and human that stand in God's path. This metaphor appears in more detail in Psalm 18:1-15, in which God, mounted on a cherub, flies in with a flurry of lightning bolts and fiery coals to rescue the psalmist (traditionally David) from his enemies. This divine warrior image often involves the conquering of the watery chaos (Pss 18:15; 74:13-15; 104:6). Here, God's drying up of the sea and the rivers is similar to well-known traditions about the Canaanite storm deity Ba'al, who conquers the violent gods named Sea and River.

Note as well that this passage suggests that God "came from Teman" and "from Mount Paran." These places are in the southern desert of Sinai and reflect an ancient tradition that Israel's God origina-206ted among the desert tribes of Sinai. Indeed, it was in this place and among these tribes that Moses met God at the burning bush (Exod 3). Some scholars have argued that Moses' theophany at Sinai reflects a shift in Israel's understanding of God from the patriarchal deity of Abraham to the warrior God of tribal Israel in Exodus-Judges. Exodus 6:2-3 even suggests that the Israelites did not know God's name to be "Yahweh" until the revelation to Moses at Sinai.

The tradition that the Lord came from the southern desert also appears in two ancient poems: Deuteronomy 33:2 says, "The LORD came from Sinai, and dawned from Seir upon us; he shone forth from Mount Paran"; Judges 5:4 says, "LORD, when you went out from Seir, when you marched from the region of Edom, the earth trembled, and the heavens poured, the clouds indeed poured water." This second verse resonates with the present theophany, in which God's procession from the wilderness has a myriad of effects on the natural and human environment. Indeed, the reaction of nature and of human enemies is of a piece. In the presence of God, the earth shakes and the nations tremble (3:6), as "in fury" God has "trod the earth" and "trampled nations" (3:12). By means of shooting arrows, God has "split the earth with rivers" (3:9) and "pierced with his own arrows the head of his warriors," thus defeating the invading army (3:14). The natural images of sun, moon, rivers, and oceans evoke the idea of God's creation of the world as a victory over chaos. This image is in concert with the creative activity of God in Genesis 1, in which God separates and divides the darkness and the waters, the primordial powers of chaos. There is a natural link, therefore, between God's creative activity in the victory over chaos and God's protective activity in defeating those who threaten God's people.

As in the story of Moses in Exodus 3 and of Isaiah (Isa 6), the vision of God's presence creates a strong physical reaction in the prophet. Habakkuk trembles and grows faint at the sight of this powerful God marching forth against enemies, and his only response is to "wait quietly for the day of calamity to come upon the people who attack us" (3:16). The focus of the prophetic book has shifted from the theological problem of wickedness in Judah, to the theological problem of God's use of wicked armies to punish Judah, and now to the theological problem of the dissonance between hope and reality. The prophet knows what has been "appointed," but for the time being matters remain very bleak for the prophet and his nation. A foreign enemy presses down upon them. Whether or not God is using that army for some larger purpose, the people's only hope of salvation lies in God's protection and mercy (3:2).

This hymn of praise shifts at the end to a thoughtful and honest reflection on the realities of enemy invasion (3:17-19). Crops will be destroyed, flocks will be killed or stolen, and the people will face the harsh realities of starvation and disease. "Yet," the prophet testifies, "I will exult in the God of my salvation" (3:18). Patient waiting and hopeful trust in God's mercy and powerful deliverance is the prophet's only consolation now.

Habbakuk marks a turning point in the prophetic tradition. The harsh and aloof condemnation of Amos has given way to sensitive *pathos* and empathetic advocacy for the weak and suffering. The moral high-mindedness of Isaiah has been tempered with honest doubt and tentative questioning of God's purposes. In the end Habakkuk affirms with Amos and Isaiah that God's pure and just purposes will be achieved, even if the realities of the world are not as neat and tidy as their theological system might imply.

Chapter 8

Jeremiah/Lamentations

Introduction

Jeremiah has been called "the weeping prophet," though the term does not nearly capture the full range of emotions in the book. To be sure, there are sections of prophetic *pathos*—confessions of sorrow about the terrible situation in Judah—but there is also much more. In addition to his sadness, readers experience Jeremiah's anger and astonishment at -206the wickedness of the people, his impatience with God for delaying the nation's judgment, and ultimately his expression of hope in God's ability to redeem and recreate Israel as God's own people.

Jeremiah ministered in Jerusalem during the chaotic final years of Judah, from the beginning of Babylonian hostilities in the last decade of the seventh century BCE to the destruction of Jerusalem by Nebuchadnezzar in 586 BCE. He shares with prophets before him the conviction that God is the Lord of history who directs and uses the actions of foreign nations for divine purposes. This theology may have seemed more palatable to the people during the ministry of some earlier prophets, when God was moving against Israel, Aram, and other Judean rivals. Jeremiah's suggestion that God has placed Nebuchadnezzar's "yoke" over the necks of Judah, and that they should cooperate with the Babylonians, makes him an unpopular figure in Jerusalem. Jeremiah declares that if the people will not listen to his counsel, Judah and her leaders will pay the ultimate price.

When Jeremiah turned out to be correct about the failure of any rebellion against Babylon, later editors preserved and extended his message so that it could address the situation of the Babylonian exiles. Jeremiah had described the exiles as the "good figs" and the basis of God's future restoration of Judah, and so his message resonated with the Babylonian exile community. Thus, while Jeremiah was supremely unwelcome in Jerusalem because of his condemnation of the Judean leadership, he became a central architect of later Israelite identity.

Historical Context

Jeremiah's ministry began during the reign of Josiah (Jer 23:3) and extended into the final governorship of Gedaliah (40:5), when he was forcibly taken with Judean refugees into Egypt (43:1-7). Living in Jerusalem during its last downward spiral, Jeremiah prophesied during the reigns of Josiah, Jehoiakim, Jehoiachin, and Zedechiah and witnessed the destruction of Jerusalem by Nebuchadnezzar in 586.

Jeremiah's earliest prophecies date from the final years of the reign of King Josiah (Jer 25:1). In 609 BCE Josiah was killed by the Egyptian pharaoh Neco, who established Egyptian dominance over Judah and installed Jehoiakim as a puppet-king. In Jeremiah 2:18 the prophet refers to Judah's previous alliances with foreign powers such as Assyria and Egypt. Now, he says, the nations on which they formerly relied have turned against them. Jeremiah goes on to predict an invasion of Judah from the north, a "boiling pot" about to spill over the land (1:13; cf. 4:6; 6:1, 22; 10:22). In this early period Jeremiah does not identify these northern invaders by name but only calls them "tribes of the kingdoms" (1:14) and "a great nation" (6:22).

It soon became clear that this northern threat was Babylon, the resurgent and powerful kingdom ruled by Nebuchadnezzar (25:9). In 605 BCE the Babylonians defeated the Egyptians and the Assyrians at Carchemish and established imperial dominance over Jehoiakim and Judah. Jeremiah calls Nebuchadnezzar God's "servant" and asserts that God has sent Nebuchadnezzar to punish Judah and all of the surrounding peoples who shall "drink from the cup" of God's judgment (25:17-29). Jeremiah directs his scribe Baruch to write this prophecy on a scroll and then read it in the hearing of the king's officials (Jer 36; cf. 45:1; 51:61-63). This message is obviously not well received by Jehoiakim. Thus Jeremiah is arrested and tried for sedition, although he is spared because of the past precedent of Micah (26:16-19). However, the text immediately notes that another prophet, Uriah, is arrested and killed for prophesying "in words exactly like those of Jeremiah" (6:20). The people are evidently persuaded that Jeremiah is a true prophet and that they might bring death upon themselves if they kill him (26:15).

Jehoiakim was not loyal to Nebuchadnezzar for long. Around 600 BCE he rebelled, which provoked a Babylonian invasion of Judah (2 Kgs 24:1-7). Before Nebuchadnezzar could make it Jerusalem, Jehoiakim died or was assassinated and was succeeded by his son Jehoiachin, also called Jeconiah (2 Kgs 24:8-9). Three months into his reign, Jehoiachin surrendered to Nebuchadnezzar and was exiled to Babylon with many members of his court and the leading citizens of Judah. Nebuchadnezzar placed the king's uncle, Mattaniah, on the throne and took the treasures from the temple and the palace as payment for his trouble.

Jeremiah 27–29 records Jeremiah's perspective on the years following Nebuchadnezzar's first invasion. Jeremiah says that God has appointed the Babylonians as overlords over Judah and that the correct path is for them to acquiesce. Jeremiah describes the exiles as "good figs" and those who remain in Judah as "bad figs" (Jer 24). This is the context for Jeremiah's conflict with the prophet Hananiah, who prophesies wrongly that the exiles and treasures will be restored within two years. Jeremiah sends a letter to the exiles, instructing them to settle down for a lifetime rather than wait for a quick restoration. Incidentally, Ezekiel was among those taken to Babylon in this first deportation. His early oracles address this same situation but from the perspective of those in exile.

Mattaniah changed his name to Zedekiah, which means "the Lord is my righteousness," an interesting claim for a ruler put on the throne by Nebuchadnezzar. Jeremiah 37–38 suggests that Zedekiah would like to heed the prophet's message of submission to Babylon but that he is forced by internal Judean politics to cooperate with the Egyptians and rebel against Babylon. Zedekiah's eventual rebellion provoked another invasion by Nebuchadnezzar in 586 BCE (2 Kgs 25; Jer 39; 52), in which the city walls were destroyed and the temple burned. Zedekiah was captured and taken to Nebuchadnezzar, who killed his sons and sent him blinded as a prisoner to Babylon. This bleak turn of events, including Zedekiah's death in captivity, is reflected in Jeremiah's prophecy in 34:1-5.

Much of the second half of Jeremiah concerns the final conflict with Babylon and the destruction of Jerusalem. He describes a city in crisis, with himself in danger because of his opposition to the court officials. For a brief time the Babylonian army withdrew because of an Egyptian army that had come out to help (Jer 37), but Jeremiah predicts correctly that the Egyptians will return home, allowing the Babylonians to continue their siege. At this time Jeremiah attempts to leave the city to purchase his ancestral property in Anatoth, but he is arrested for deserting to the enemy (37:11-16). Zedekiah spares his life, but he remains in prison for the remainder of the invasion. In the chaotic final days Jeremiah is taken by officials from prison and thrown into a muddy cistern to die (38:5-6). Zedekiah, however, sends instructions for him to be rescued from the pit and protects Jeremiah from his rivals for the remainder of the siege.

When the city fell, Nebuchadnezzar installed Gedaliah as the governor of Judah, now a Babylonian territory rather than an independent nation, but he was soon assassinated by the murderous insurrectionist Ishmael (Jer 41:2). The book of Jeremiah says that the prophet is initially taken with Judean captives bound for Babylon but that he is released with an invitation to live freely in Babylon or else to return to

JEREMIAH/LAMENTATIONS

Jerusalem, which he does (40:1-6). Fearing Babylonian reprisals for the murder of Gedaliah, a number of Judeans flee to Egypt, taking Jeremiah with them (42:1–43:7). The nation of Judah is now gone, and there is no record of prophetic activity in the land until the Persian restoration fifty years later.

Theological Traditions

Our study began with Amos, the prophetic book with the purest theology of judgment. Now, we turn to Jeremiah, the prophet who integrates God's judgment with a creative and powerful theology of redemption.

Drawing upon the tradition of the conditional covenantal, Amos had argued that the people's sins had severed their bond with God and that they would be utterly destroyed. Later prophets developed a tentative hope for the redemption of Israel and Judah and expressed their hope that a faithful remnant would become the basis for a restored community. Isaiah in particular drew upon "Zion theology" to affirm that God would honor the ancient promises to David by bringing about a renewed Davidic kingdom that will reign in peace from Jerusalem. The Davidic covenant, as expressed in 2 Samuel 7 and other texts, made eternal promises to David without any legal stipulations. Thus, there was a tension between the *conditional* covenant language of Amos, which drew on the Mosaic tradition, and the *unconditional* covenant language of Isaiah. The judgment oracles in Isaiah and Micah stop short of predicting total annihilation and instead characterize the judgment as either a corrective warning from God or even the tragic result of bad leadership in the political and religious realms. If the covenant cannot be broken, then Israel and Judah's sin cannot lead to God's final rejection of the people. Furthermore, since God resides on Mount Zion (Jerusalem), then the city itself must be invulnerable to attack.

Jeremiah is the first prophetic book to integrate the Mosaic and Davidic traditions thoroughly. Of course, it is difficult to differentiate the passages that come from the historical figure of Jeremiah from those of later editors. It may be that the full expression of Davidic hope comes from an exilic editorial layer, as we see in Amos and Hosea. However, there is enough theological complexity in the book to suggest that Jeremiah himself brought the full range of theological traditions to bear upon Judah's changing situation.

In our discussion of theological traditions in this book thus far, we have focused primarily on ideas and images related to God's judgment. This section will highlight three theological topics related to the theology of God's mercy and salvation. First, Jeremiah communicates the emotional anguish of God's judgment more than any prophet before him. Earlier, we saw a few passages expressing prophetic empathy or *pathos*, such as the lament of Habakkuk (1:2-4), Micah's sorrow for the poor who are devoured by the rich (3:1-3), and Hosea's quotation of God saying "How can I give you up, Ephraim?" (11:8). In Jeremiah, the emotional effects of judgment prophecy are even more evident. In a series of "confessions," he laments the suffering of Judah as well as his own persecution. In 5:18 he calls his pain "unceasing" and "incurable" and accuses God of being like a deceitful "wadi," a stream bed that dries up in the summer when water is needed the most. Likewise, in 20:7 Jeremiah accuses God of overpowering his own free will and forcing him to deliver an odious message of judgment. He feels sorrow at the pain of his people, prays in lamentation "Is there no balm in Gilead?" and weeps "day and night for the slain of my poor people" (8:22–9:1). Jeremiah describes the confusion and dismay of people during a terrible drought and asks God plaintively, "Why should you be like a stranger in the land . . . like a mighty warrior who cannot give help?" (14:8-9). If God is the Lord of all history, there is danger in seeing divine power as an aloof and cruelly inexorable force that does as it wills without concern for its effect on the world. Such a sovereign and capricious God would be the tyrant described by Job: "He snatches away; who can stop him? Who will say to him, 'What are you doing?'" (Job 9:12). In his honest questioning, Jeremiah affirms the lordship of God without elevating it to such a barbarous abstraction.

Second, Jeremiah says that the Babylonian exile is only part of God's plan, a time of preparation for a glorious and prosperous future. In chapter 24 he says that the two groups of Judeans—those left in Jerusalem and those taken to Babylon—are like two baskets of figs, one ripe and one rotten. The exiles to Babylon are the "good figs" (24:5), whom God will restore to the land to build up and plant again (24:6). Echoing the language of Hosea, Jeremiah says that this righteous remnant will "return" to God and once again "shall be my people and I will be their God" (24:7). This identification of the good and bad "figs" is naturally the exact opposite of the view held by his Jerusalem audience. Surely the people taken to Babylon are the ones being judged by God while the favored ones are being spared at home. Jeremiah reverses this natural assumption and sets the groundwork for the remainder of the prophetic (and biblical) tradition by tying the hope of Israel's restoration to the fate of the Babylonian exiles.

Third, Jeremiah emphasizes the role of God's anointed ruler, the "messiah." Like other eighth-century prophets, Jeremiah attributes much of Judah's suffering to the selfishness and incompetence of its political and religious leadership. The "shepherds" of the people, he says, are "stupid" (10:21) and have trampled down God's pleasant vineyard (12:10). They are the ones responsible for the scattering of the people, the "sheep" of God's pasture (23:2). Jeremiah says that in the future, God will raise up good shepherds for the people (23:4). God will also anoint a king in the line of David who will "reign as king and deal wisely, and shall execute justice and righteousness in the land" (23:5; cf. 30:9; 33:15). In chapter 33 Jeremiah describes the rebuilding and renewed glory of future Jerusalem, ruled over by a righteous "branch" of David. He says that there will always be a king in Jerusalem in fulfillment of the unconditional Davidic covenant. The promises to David, he says, are as reliable as the rising and setting of the sun (33:20). It is on this basis that Judah can trust in the promise of God, who says, "I will restore their fortunes, and will have mercy upon them" (33:26).

Literary Features

The literary composition of Jeremiah is exceptionally complex. The book underwent a series of significant additions and revisions over the years, seen for example in the fact that the Greek version of the book in the Septuagint is one-eighth shorter, with a different order of materials after chapter 25. Whether the Greek translators used a shorter Hebrew text than the one represented by the Hebrew Bible or abridged the text in their translation is unclear. Both long and shorter versions of the Hebrew textual tradition are attested among the Dead Sea Scrolls found at Qumran.

There are three types of material found in the book: (a) poetic oracles, similar in style and form to the judgment and salvation oracles found in earlier prophets; (b) long prose sermons that the prophet delivers in oral and written form to his audience; and (c) historical narratives that may be described as "prophetic reports." These different genres of prophetic text provide a glimpse into the redactional history of the book.

For example, the famous "temple sermon" appears in a long prose narrative in chapter 7 and also in a shorter form as part of a prophetic report in Jeremiah 26:1-6. The second passage leads directly into Jeremiah's arrest and trial for sedition while the longer version leads into vivid poetic descriptions of invasion and the violent destruction of Jerusalem. Many scholars consider the longer version to be a later expansion of the original shorter text. Even if that is the case, however, why would the final editors include both rather than simply expanding the one in chapter 26? And why would they be separated by two dozen chapters of other material? Also, there seems to be some theological development from the shorter passage to the longer one. In Jeremiah 26:3 God tells the prophet to warn the people about the possibility of God's judgment so they might turn back to God and avoid the punishment. If they will not listen, he says, then the temple will be "like Shiloh." In 7:13-15, however, God emphasizes that the people have stubbornly refused to listen to warnings;

thus, God will do to the temple "just what I did to Shiloh." God tells Jeremiah to give the sermon to the people, "but they will not listen to you." The prophecy is more of an announcement than a warning and makes the most sense as a postdestruction reflection on Judah's disregard for Jeremiah's warning message.

Some of the most intriguing passages in the book are the prose narratives that describe Jeremiah's literary process. Jeremiah writes a letter to the Babylonian exiles that is preserved in Jeremiah 29. The references to specific leaders in Babylon and Jerusalem in 29:24-32 suggest that this could be an actual letter composed for the occasion. In Jeremiah 36 he dictates a scroll to his scribe Baruch and has him read it in the hearing of the royal officials. King Jehoiakim has the scroll read to him, and he burns it in his fire piece by piece (36:23), but Jeremiah dictates a new scroll (36:28) to which "many similar words were added" (36:32). Finally, in Jeremiah 51:29-63 the prophet sends a scroll with a person traveling from Egypt to Babylon, with instructions to read the oracle in Babylon, "tie a stone to it, and throw it into the middle of the Euphrates." The process of writing, editing, and augmenting the prophecy began with the prophet himself, though it continued for generations to come.

The narratives *about* the prophet do not appear to be written by the prophet himself but are based on oral tradition or perhaps on records kept by Baruch. One surprising element of these prophetic reports is how wide-ranging they are. We hear about Jeremiah's legal troubles and persecution. We are privy to secret meetings with the king, including one conversation that Jeremiah specifically covers up with a lie (38:24-28). We learn that Nebuchadnezzar gives Jeremiah an opportunity to live in peaceful asylum in Babylon (40:1-6) and witness his conflict with obstinate Judean women in the Egyptian diaspora (Jer 44).

How these traditions traveled from place to place and eventually came together is unknown. In the final form of the text, however, prophetic report narratives serve an important literary purpose—that of providing an internal context for interpreting the prophet's oracles. Jeremiah's oracles against the priests and officials of Judah have more rhetorical effect when read in light of the prophet's persecution at their hands. The idea that the righteous remnant will emerge from Babylon and not Egypt finds a concrete footing in the narratives about the Judeans who ignore Jeremiah's advice, force him to go with them to Egypt, and then continue to transgress God's religious requirements (Jer 42–44).

The literary style of Jeremiah is shaped by the book's use of the "grand metaphor," broad attempts to describe the people's situation that border on allegory. For example, Jeremiah 24 compares the Judeans to two baskets of figs, one good and one bad. Another example of the grand metaphor is Jeremiah's comparison of God with a potter who makes a vessel that turns out wrong. The potter, he says, is free to destroy the vessel and use the clay as part of a new vessel. If the people do not change their ways, God says, "I am a potter shaping evil against you" (18:11). The pottery metaphor is emphasized rhetorically through two actions: Jeremiah delivers this message in the context of actually visiting a potter's studio, and he later smashes a clay jug to illustrate God's violent destruction of Judah (19:1-15). Significantly, this oracle and pottery smashing takes place beside the valley of Hinnom, the site of the religious abominations that he is denouncing, but also the "entry of the Potsherd Gate" (19:2). The prophet coordinates the words that he speaks, the things that he does, and the places in which these prophetic acts take place.

This same coordination is seen in Jeremiah's use of "yoke" imagery to describe God's exercise of divine authority over the people. In 2:20 the people break their yoke and declare that they "will not serve!" Jeremiah says that in response to the people's disobedience, God has placed the yoke of the king of Babylon over them. Any nation who peacefully submits to the dominance of Nebuchadnezzar will be spared, but any nation—including Judah—that resists will be crushed. Jeremiah wears a wooden yoke on his shoulders in order to demonstrate this message (Jer 27). When Hananiah prophesies that God has "broken the yoke of the king of Babylon"

(28:1), Jeremiah confronts him with his own message of a long exile. The other prophet breaks Jeremiah's wooden yoke, but Jeremiah responds with the prophecy that "you have broken wooden bars only to forge iron bars in place of them" (28:13).

Commentary

Jeremiah 1–10

The book begins with a "call narrative" in which Jeremiah says that God had chosen him to be a prophet even before his birth and called him to that vocation as a youth. God overcomes Jeremiah's objection that he is "only a boy" with the promise to send him to the right places with the right words in his mouth. Reminiscent of Isaiah's mouth purification, Jeremiah says that "the LORD put out his hand and touched my mouth" (1:9; cf. Ezek 3:1-3). Whereas Isaiah is told to confuse his audience, Jeremiah is given power "to pluck up and to pull down, to destroy and to overthrow, to build and to plant" (1:10). These words appear many times in the book and relate to God's power over the world's peoples to punish and reward them as they deserve (6:15; 8:12; 11:17; 12:14; 18:7-9; 24:6; 31:28; 32:41; 42:10; 45:4). God has endowed Jeremiah with divine prophetic authority to announce these momentous actions of God.

Similar to God warning Ezekiel that he will be held responsible for the people's sin if he does not accurately deliver the prophetic warning (Ezek 3:20-21), Jeremiah is told that if he "breaks" in front of the people and fails to speak the prophecy, God will "break" him. God compares Jeremiah to city fortifications that will stand against all attacks, which turns out to be a quality that he desperately needs (1:18; 15:19-21; cf. Ezek 3:8-9). In Jeremiah 20 we will see that Jeremiah is indeed brought to the very breaking point in his ministry.

Given the length and complexity of this book, it is impossible to provide comment about every oracle or interesting motif. However, we can identify several important ideas that run through each section of the book. In this early material delivered before Nebuchadnezzar's first invasion, Jeremiah paints a vivid picture of judgment upon the people of Judah. He draws upon prophetic metaphors developed by the eighth-century prophets and reinterprets them for his own late Judean context.

First, Jeremiah compares Judah's religious idolatry to the sexual immorality of an adulterous bride, similar to many passages in Hosea. He says that Judah had been an innocent bride in her youth in the wilderness, but now she has turned away from God and toward Baal and other gods (2:7-8, 13). Jeremiah describes a variety of illegitimate religious practices such as worshiping at open-air altars, called "high places," an activity that he compares to having illicit sex "on every high hill and under every green tree" (2:20; 3:6). He mentions two specific objects used in these outdoor shrines: sacred trees and stone pillars (2:26; 3:9). These objects are the "asherah pole," a wooden fertility symbol, and the "masseba," a stone symbol of male potency, and both are attested in archaeological and epigraphic evidence from Judean sites. Jeremiah says that families work together to make cakes for the queen of heaven, a reference to one of the fertility goddesses of the ancient world, probably Astarte (7:18). These practices take place in the countryside and in homes and represent aspects of "popular piety" in Judah that often conflicted with the official theology promoted from Jerusalem. However, Jeremiah also says that the Jerusalem worship is corrupt, with people putting "abominations" in the temple and possibly practicing human sacrifice on the Tophet altar just outside the city (7:30-32; see the discussion of 19:56). These practices are all mentioned as targets of the reforms of Josiah in 2 Kings 23:1-14.

Jeremiah compares these activities to sexual promiscuity, saying that the people are consumed by lust like wild animals in heat (2:24). Their wicked behavior is matched by their arrogant self-deception. Several times, Jeremiah includes a "rhetorical quotation" from people who refuse to recognize their own guilt or danger of punishment. The people say, "We are free" (2:31), asserting their independence from divine authority like the libertine citizens of Israel in Hosea 10:3.

They declare that God "will do nothing" (5:12) about their sins, so they "will not give heed" (6:16-17) to the warnings of the prophets. They declare in the temple that "we are safe" even while they are in danger of judgment (7:10) and deceive themselves with the affirmation that "we are wise, and the law of the LORD is with us" (8:8). The people are all guilty, both rich and poor alike, and all deserve the judgment that is coming. The priests and prophets have failed in their duty to warn and lead the people (6:13-15; 8:10-12), and the people would not even listen to the words they did hear (6:16-17).

Second, Jeremiah describes the coming invasion in highly descriptive and emotionally powerful terms. There are several visions in this section of invasion from the north (4:5-18; 5:14-17; 6:21-30; 8:14-17). He does not mention Babylon by name here, and expects not a single foe but many (1:15). Jeremiah compares this invading army with a lion on the hunt (4:7; 5:6), a swift wind or eagles (4:13), and poisonous snakes loose in the city (8:7). His description of siege warfare is remarkably accurate, with references to refugees hiding in the hills (4:29), siege ramps (6:6), armies camped around the city (4:17; 6:3), and the devastating effects on the city, including famine (5:17), ecological disaster (9:10), poisoned water (9:15), and poor health (8:22). In verse 19:9 Jeremiah predicts that the siege will force the starving people into cannibalism.

Along with these intense descriptions of violence, Jeremiah goes further than any other prophet in expressing his anguish at the terrible situation in which his people have put themselves: "My anguish! I writhe in pain! Oh, the walls of my heart! My heart is beating wildly; I cannot keep silent; for I hear the sound of the trumpet, the alarm of war" (4:19). As a prophet, he knows what is about to happen, but the people are acting like "stupid children" who only do what is wrong (4:22; 10:21). Although he feels justified in his frustration and anger at the people, he does not find any dark pleasure in their pain. His "heart is sick" with grief (8:18) and his eyes full of tears of lamentation (9:1, 18).

Third, in the famous "temple sermon" in chapter 7, Jeremiah explains the coming judgment in covenantal terms (cf. 11:1-8). He says the people come into the temple in Jerusalem with a deceptive belief in their own righteousness and an irrational confidence that they will be safe. He says to those worshiping in Jerusalem that they should not "trust in these deceptive words: 'This is the temple of the LORD'" (7:4). This is a reference to the Zion theology tradition that God has chosen Jerusalem as the place of his dwelling. It is likely that the Assyrian king Sennacherib's inability to conquer the city in 701 BCE (through God's intervention, according to 2 Kgs 19:35-36) had convinced the people that Jerusalem was not vulnerable to attack.

Jeremiah says that the promises of the (unconditional) Zion tradition cannot outweigh the requirements of the (conditional) Sinai covenant. In 7:9 he accuses the people of breaking half of the Ten Commandments while they continue worshiping in the temple and saying, "We are safe." Just as God had destroyed Israel for its sins, so Judah can also be judged, regardless of the special status of Jerusalem as God's dwelling (7:12-15). Ezekiel takes this idea even further in his vision of God's mobile throne (Ezek 1) that is lifted out of Jerusalem as God burns down the city (Ezek 10). As we saw in the "Theological Traditions" section, both Jeremiah and Ezekiel consider the Babylonian exiles to be the righteous remnant. Being in Jerusalem is no guarantee of God's protection, and exile from Jerusalem does not mean God cannot be present among the community.

Because the worshipers in Jerusalem have neglected the important ethical requirements of the covenant, their sacrifices and offerings are not acceptable to God (6:20). Jeremiah goes so far as to suggest that God had not even asked for sacrificial offerings before the people settled in the land (7:22-26), which may indicate that Jeremiah did not have access to the priestly legislation in Exodus–Numbers. God will not honor the requests made by this people, but Jeremiah is instructed not to intercede on their behalf (7:16; 11:14; 14:11). Their relationship with God has been profoundly severed. This is not a welcome message in Jerusalem. Another version of the temple sermon is found in Jeremiah 26:1-6, it leads to the prophet's arrest and trial for sedition.

Jeremiah 11–20

This section of Jeremiah focuses mostly on the complex relationship that Jeremiah has with his community, with God, and with the prophetic message itself. He is charged with delivering a message that causes him pain just to think about coming true and then causes him pain when it is delayed in its fulfillment. He stands with his people in yearning for health and justice and peace but denounces them for their wickedness, arrogance, and petty scheming. God has empowered Jeremiah to deliver the message and protected him from his enemies, but in his darkest moments Jeremiah feels violated by God. In this discussion we will look at Jeremiah's interactions with the people and at his internal experience of being a prophet.

As discussed in the Introduction, it is important to remember that we cannot reconstruct the psychology or biography of the prophet, though Jeremiah does contain the most information of that type. These texts are not part of Jeremiah's diary or private journal. Even the intimate-sounding revelations of the prophet's thoughts and emotions are part of the public rhetoric of "Jeremiah," the literary character constructed by the book in its final form. Although we will talk about Jeremiah's statements and feelings, we should give the most attention to how these personal statements support and convey the prophet's public message.

The first aspect of Jeremiah's experience is that being a prophet of judgment is a profoundly difficult calling. In chapter 16 God tells Jeremiah that he is not permitted to have a wife or family (16:1) or to lament the terrible sufferings that lie in wait for the people or to mourn with those whose family have died (16:5-8).

The message itself is difficult to manage, and Jeremiah alternates between expressions of sorrow at the suffering of the people and intensely violent descriptions of their destruction. In chapter 14, for example, he provides an empathetic vision of the suffering of the people during a drought (vv. 1-6). The people are lying in gloom and dismay at the lack of water, with even the wild animals suffering in the wilderness for lack of food. Jeremiah speaks on behalf of the people and asks God to send relief, to be the "hope of Israel, its savior in time of trouble" (14:8). He quotes the words of the people to God, asking, "Have you completely rejected Judah? Does your heart loathe Zion?" (14:19). Unlike some earlier sarcastic quotes, this one seems to be a genuine question, and in response God tells Jeremiah to tell the people that those who are "destined for pestilence," the sword, famine, and captivity will have it (15:2). He is not given space to mourn for the people or to intercede for them.

To a people in crisis, Jeremiah preaches a message of violent judgment, using a variety of disturbing metaphors. He says that God is about to make everyone succumb to drunkenness so they will fall and be destroyed: "And I will dash them one against another, parents and children together, says the LORD. I will not pity or spare or have compassion when I destroy them" (13:13-14). The people stumble around and finally succumb to darkness while Jeremiah weeps "in secret" (13:16-17). Evoking the punishment of the faithless wife in Hosea 2, and perhaps extending the metaphor of the effects of drunkenness, Jeremiah says that the people will be like a woman stripped and raped by her enemies (13:22) and that God will be the one to lift up the skirts (13:26). He describes the invasion of Jerusalem as having three stages: that of the swords that kill, the dogs that drag out the bodies, and the birds and animals that eat the carcasses (15:3).

These terrible images of judgment are rivaled, however, by Jeremiah's insinuation that the Judeans have practiced the worst possible abominations in the valley outside Jerusalem: child sacrifice. In chapter 19 he goes in the valley of Hinnom, the traditional site of the "Topheth" altar and denounces this place of illegitimate worship. He says in v. 5 that they "burn their children in the fire as burnt offerings to Baal" and that soon the whole city will be like the Topheth; defiled and filled with dead bodies (19:13). Such a dark and twisted prophecy can only be a response to a dark and twisted community, thoroughly corrupt. But to say such words and to think such thoughts exact a heavy toll on the mental well-being of the prophet.

A second aspect of Jeremiah's experience as a prophet is that his political opponents in Jerusalem are constantly conspiring against him. These schemes have been revealed to him by God (11:18-19), so he calls down God's retribution on his enemies (11:20). God claims to have intervened to help him (15:11), but Jeremiah evidently feels that God has not done enough because he continues to plead with God to do something about them (15:15-18). He had willingly taken on the prophetic task, but now he feels abandoned, alone, and in unceasing pain.

One problem is that even though Jeremiah has delivered the terrible prophecy of judgment, the predicted invasion has not occurred. Jeremiah prophesied doom against the house of Zedekiah from its first year (27:1), and as the years passed, it must have seemed that Jeremiah was a false prophet. His opponents say to him, "Where is the word of the LORD? Let it come!" (17:15). In 15:18 Jeremiah makes an astonishing comparison between God and a *wadi*, a seasonal stream bed in the desert that is dry during summer months. Jeremiah says that God is like "a deceitful brook, like waters that fail" (15:18). God responds by echoing the divine promise from 1:18 that Jeremiah will be a fortified wall, impervious to attack (15:20). It is clear, however, that Jeremiah does not feel impervious. Opponents continually plot against him (18:18), which leads Jeremiah to call upon God for protection and vindication. He says, "Let my persecutors be shamed. . . . Bring on them the day of disaster; destroy them with double destruction!" (17:18). Jeremiah asks God to starve their children, kill their young men, make their women into widows (18:21), and to "deal with them while you are angry" (18:23). The personal distress of the prophet turns him from compassion to unbridled wrath, a process that mirrors God's own exasperation with the people. Jeremiah cannot rightly question God's justice when he himself lapses into visions of dead children and widowed mothers.

Jeremiah 20 contains the most notorious of the personal experiences described by the prophet. He has a conflict with a local priest named Pashur, who physically strikes Jeremiah and receives a personalized judgment in return (cf. Amos 7:10-17). This leads directly into a personal complaint in which Jeremiah accuses God of "enticing" and "overpowering" him, verbs that when used together imply violent seduction and intimate violation (20:7). He has become a "laughingstock" because his prophecy of judgment has not come to pass, which is the very definition of a false prophet in Deuteronomy 18:22: "If a prophet speaks in the name of the LORD but the thing does not take place or prove true, it is a word that the LORD has not spoken."

The problem is that Jeremiah cannot stop himself from speaking these prophetic words. He says they are like "a burning fire shut up within my bones," and he cannot physically keep them inside. He asserts that if God gives him a message of judgment but then delays in sending the judgment, then it is God's fault that people plot against him. Jeremiah curses the day of his birth (20:14), saying it would have been better if he had been stillborn: "Why did I come forth from the womb to see toil and sorrow, and spend my days in shame?" (20:18).

So why does Jeremiah include such personal and painful "confessions"? One reason is that the personal struggle of the prophet rhetorically validates his message. There is always a suspicion that a prophet might speak a word in support of his own interests. This seems to be behind Amos's statement that he is "no prophet, nor a prophet's son" (7:14, i.e., not a professional prophet), an assurance to the people that he is just delivering a message, not looking for any type of material gain. If the prophecy is difficult for Jeremiah, both because he is grieved at Judah's situation and because it makes him a target of opposition, then the people should pay closer attention to what he says. In other words, why would anyone invent such a prophecy? Jeremiah says that the hearers should trust him; he would not say these things unless he absolutely *had* to.

JEREMIAH / LAMENTATIONS

Jeremiah 21–31

This middle section of Jeremiah centers around two basic issues. First, the prophet addresses specific prophecies to the royal house and reflects more broadly about the nature of good and bad leadership. Second, Jeremiah looks beyond the now-beginning exile to the time of future restoration. When will it be, and what is required for it to happen?

Jeremiah 21 narrates an event that takes place during the second invasion of Nebuchadnezzar in 586 BCE. In the midst of this catastrophe, King Zedekiah sends a message to Jeremiah, asking him to intercede on behalf of the people. (Notice that one of the messengers is the aforementioned Passhur.) Jeremiah responds with a characteristically negative oracle, saying that God has given Zedekiah and the whole city into the hands of Nebuchadnezzar, who "shall not pity them, or spare them, or have compassion" (21:7). As it happens, though, they have one last chance for survival, a choice between "the way of life and the way of death" (21:8-9). Anyone who stays in the city will be killed, as previously predicted, but anyone who goes into the field and surrenders to Nebuchadnezzar will be spared and taken to Babylon alive. The story does not narrate the king's response, but it is not hard to imagine.

This narrative leads directly into a reflection on the nature of good royal leadership. A king is required to execute justice and protect the weak and oppressed (21:12). The king should embody the principles of justice and righteousness and defend the alien, orphan, widow, and all who are vulnerable and innocent (22:2-4). Jeremiah says that if the kings rule in this way, then they will always have a throne in Jerusalem, but if they fail in this, the house of David "shall become a desolation" (22:5).

Jeremiah accuses King Jehoiakim specifically of being more concerned about his own lavish lifestyle than about his covenantal obligation to defend the weak. Jehoiakim has built and furnished a large house for himself but refuses to pay his workers (22:13-14), and Jeremiah taunts him with the question "Are you a king because you compete in cedar?" (22:15).

His father, Josiah, was a good king, concerned about justice and righteousness, but Jehoiakim has turned to oppression and violence. Therefore, Jeremiah says, the king will be killed and buried like a donkey, merely cast away without mourning (22:18-19).

Jehoiakim died in 597 BCE during the first siege of Nebuchadnezzar and was succeeded for a brief time by his son Jehoiachin, called both Jeconiah and Coniah in the text. In 22:24 Jeremiah predicts that God will turn Jehoiachin over to Nebuchadnezzar and that he will be taken into exile, cast away like a broken pot, and become the end of the royal line (22:30).

Jeremiah laments the state of leadership in Judah in general, declaring "woe to the shepherd who destroy and scatter the sheep of my pasture" (23:1). The land is full of unrighteousness while the prophets and priests have themselves turned to wickedness rather than taught and led (23:11). The prophets have offered oracles from Baal (23:13), engaged in sexual immorality, and will be destroyed like Sodom and Gomorrah (23:14).

The ineptness of Judah's leadership figures dramatically in the aftermath of Jeremiah's "temple sermon" in 26:1-6 (a brief parallel to 7:1-15). He is arrested on charges of sedition against the king and city. The officials, priests, and prophets consult on the matter and decide to spare him because of the prior example of Micah (26:16-19). However, the text immediately reports that another prophet, Uriah, was arrested and killed for the same message. The leadership of Judah is corrupt and self-centered, but they are also capricious, inept, and foolish. They are a major reason why the nation is under threat of destruction.

The second major emphasis of this section is the extent and duration of the judgment that has already begun. Many of the leading Judean people have already been taken to Babylon in 597 BCE, and a major question in Jerusalem at the time was whether the situation would improve and how quickly. Jeremiah describes the two communities, one in Jerusalem and one in Babylon, as two baskets of figs, one good and one bad (ch. 24). One would expect the "good" figs to be the people who had been "spared" in the first invasion of Nebuchadnezzar. However, Jeremiah says that the exiles are the preferred group, now set aside from the wide-reaching destruction that is coming (25:17-26). In chapter 27 Jeremiah wears a yoke into the temple as a visual symbol for his message that the Judeans had been put under the control of Babylon. In chapter 28 he has a major confrontation with another prophet, Hananiah, who was preaching that the exiles would be returned in two years (28:3-4), including King Jehoiachin. Opposed to this, Jeremiah says that the exile will last for seventy years (25:11; 29:10) and that Hananiah is a false prophet who will die within a year. Jeremiah's prophecy is confirmed (28:16-17), although it has no effect on the ongoing foreign policy of the ruling house. As Zedekiah continues to follow a policy of resistance to the Babylonians, Jeremiah sends a letter to the exiles, instructing them to settle down, get on with their lives in Babylon, and not listen to the prophets who predict a quick return (29:4-9).

What will happen at the end of the seventy-year period? In a series of oracles that probably derive from the later exilic period, Jeremiah paints a picture of a restored, redeemed, and unified Israel. God says through the prophet, "I know the plans I have for you . . . plans for your welfare and not for harm, to give you a future with hope. Then when you call upon me and come and pray to me, I will hear you" (29:11-12). Thus, the hope of Judah lies in their repentance and in God's mercy and power to redeem. The prophet describes the breaking of the "yoke" of Babylon and a restored and blessed community that includes both former Israel and Judah (30:8). Jeremiah predicts the return of exiles of Israel/Jacob (30:10; 31:7-11) and promises the return of health to Judah/Zion (30:17). The restoration and reunification of Israel is a theme in the Judean prophets as far back as Isaiah, who predicted a return to the glories of the united kingdom (Isa 7:17). Although Israel's punishment had been just, now they have asked for forgiveness (31:18-20). God's faithfulness to Israel wins out over divine wrath because, he says, "Ephraim is my firstborn" (31:9) and "the child I delight in" (31:20). Jeremiah also expresses a new idea in biblical theology: that people are responsible for their own sins rather than having to pay for the sins of their parents (31:29; cf. Ezek 18:2). This idea is important to the hope of the exilic community, now the children and grandchildren of those originally taken to Babylon.

The reunified people will have their own rulers, not foreign-imposed puppets (30:18). Israel will be united with Judah not merely politically but, more importantly, in their shared worship in Jerusalem. The northern sentinels will say, "Come, let us go up to Zion, to the LORD our God" (31:6), and the peoples from both north and south "shall be radiant over the goodness of the LORD" (31:12). This blessed community is summed up with the statement from God that "you shall be my people, and I will be your God" (30:22). In this new situation God will recreate the covenant that had been broken, and this new covenant will be more effective than the first because now the people will have God's Law written "on their hearts" rather than having it merely mediated through teachers and leaders (31:31-34).

Notice that the "new covenant" is not a resumption of the old but something genuinely new and also that it is still structurally "conditional," like the Mosaic covenant. The old covenant had been totally broken, and Israel/Judah could not reasonably expect any more opportunities to live in community with God. This new chance is due to God's commitment to the line of David. God will raise up "for David" a new king, called "a righteous branch," who will govern in the way that only David had done (23:5; 33:14-26). The same term had been used by Isaiah to describe the coming anointed ruler of Judah, the "branch" or "shoot" that shall come from the stump of Jesse (Isa 11:1; cf. Mic 5:2). This developing "messianic" tradition in the prophets grows out of the Judean royal theology, centered on Zion, David, and temple, and continues to develop in new ways in the history of ancient Judaism through the first century CE. For more on the appropriation of this tradition by New Testament writers, see the Conclusion chapter.

JEREMIAH/LAMENTATIONS

Jeremiah 32–45

This section of Jeremiah consists mainly of prose narrative that describes events in Jeremiah's ministry as well as the final days of Judah's national existence. The order is not historical, so readers must pay attention to the contextual clues and introductory phrases for each chapter. The central purpose of the section is to show that the Judean leadership had ample warning to avoid the catastrophe that followed their decision to rebel against the Babylonians, even in the very final days of Nebuchadnezzar's assault. Also, those who avoid capture consider themselves to be a righteous remnant, but their decision to flee to Egypt and continue their religious apostasy cuts them off from any future Judean restoration.

In the early days of his ministry, Jeremiah has an encounter with a group of "Rechabites," followers of a strict religious sect (ch. 35). Jeremiah is impressed with their faithful adherence to their religious orders and contrasts their obedience to difficult laws with the people's refusal to follow the much easier law of God (35:14). The Rechabites are rewarded with a promise of perpetual lineage (35:18-19) while the Judeans will receive "every disaster that I have pronounced against them" (35:17). The book emphasizes the refusal of the Judeans to listen by following this story with a narrative showing the refusal of Jehoiakim to heed the clear prophecy of Jeremiah. In chapter 36 Jeremiah dictates a scroll to his scribe Baruch and has him read it in the temple court. The royal officials who hear it know they must inform the king of this message, but before they do so, they advise Baruch and Jeremiah to hide. King Jehoiakim hears the prophecy of judgment, burns it in his fireplace, and orders the arrest of Baruch and Jeremiah (36:23, 26). Jeremiah responds with a new scroll, predicting that Jehoiakim will be killed and his body cast into the open air with no heir (36:30). These narratives establish that the Judeans were adequately warned for years before their final destruction, and at the highest levels.

Other than these two early stories, the narratives in this section date to the final months and days of Judah in 586 BCE.

Much of the story revolves around a piece of ancestral property that Jeremiah buys in his hometown of Anathoth (32:6-15). Jeremiah is in prison, and Nebuchadnezzar is besieging the city when a message arrives from his relatives asking him to buy the property. As a business decision, buying the land is sheer madness. With Babylonian control of Judah, such land ownership would mean nothing. The situation is reminiscent of an episode of *Little House on the Prairie* ("The Inheritance") in which Pa receives a large inheritance from a relative, which turns out to be a box of worthless Confederate scrip. From an outside perspective Jeremiah's investment is worthless. However, the prophet says that his purchase of the land is a sign that Judah will be restored and that "fields shall be bought in this land" (32:43) in the future. The book contrasts Jeremiah's honorable purchase of property with the unjust treatment of Judean slaves during this time (34:8-22). Zedekiah had legally released the Judean slaves, whom the laws state must be released every seven years, but then the people reneged on the release and took them as slaves again (34:16). Now, God will "release" them—"to the sword, to pestilence, and to famine" (34:17).

When Jeremiah attempts to leave the city to claim his property, he is arrested for suspected desertion to the Babylonians (37:13). Jeremiah tells Zedekiah that he, Zedekiah, will be handed over to the Babylonians but, even so, asks the king to spare him from prison. Zedekiah has him confined in the comparatively comfortable court of the guard (37:21). Zedekiah does not have complete control over his court, however, and hands Jeremiah over to officials, who throw him into a muddy cistern. Jeremiah is saved by Ebed-melech the Ethiopian, who convinces the king to spare Jeremiah; he pulls the prophet out of the cistern and restores him to the court of the guard instead of the jail (38:7-13; see also 39:15-18 and the promise of safety for Ebed-melech because of his service to Jeremiah). Jeremiah tells Zedekiah that there exists one last chance for his survival and for that of his nation: to surrender to Nebuchadnezzar (38:17; cf. 21:9). Zedekiah says that he cannot do this because he is afraid of reprisals from the Judeans who have deserted already, so Jeremiah predicts that he shall be taken and the city burned with fire (38:23).

Soon, the city does fall, Zedekiah is captured trying to flee, and the king is blinded and taken to Babylon after his sons are killed in front of him (39:1-10). Jeremiah is released to return to Jerusalem under the aegis of the new governor, Gedaliah (39:14). It is significant that the Babylonians offered Jeremiah the opportunity to come to Babylon and live freely as an honored guest (40:4). In the context of the book, this reinforces the divine favor on Jeremiah because of his faithful service and the fact that the destruction of God's punishment on wicked Judah had now occurred (cf. the Babylonian captain's statement of this in 40:2-3). However, from a political perspective, what makes Nebuchadnezzar look kindly on Jeremiah is the same thing that leads the Judean officials to imprison him: he appears objectively to be on the Babylonian side. The only thing that saves Jeremiah from death both early and late in his ministry is that people regard him as an authentic prophet, but as one with problematic political views.

The political divide between Jeremiah and his compatriots is evident even after the Babylonian conquest. The group of Judeans who remain in the land ask him to counsel them about their plan to flee to Egypt (42:1-6). Jeremiah's message is that the Judeans should wait in the land and form the basis of God's future plans for the nation (42:1-10). God promises, he says, to "build you up and not pull you down . . . plant you, and not pluck you up" (42:10), a reference to Jeremiah's commissioning in 1:10. The Judeans are afraid of the Babylonians, however, because the insurgent Ishmael, son of Nethaniah, had assassinated the governor, Gedaliah, and many others (ch. 41). They turn on Jeremiah, accuse him of lying (43:2), and forcibly take him to Egypt with them.

Jeremiah proves to be a gadfly in Egypt as well, offering a final series of denunciations of the Egyptian contingent of Judeans in chapters 43–44. He buries stones under the pavement of the pharaoh's palace and predicts that Nebuchadnezzar would build his throne over those stones (43:8-12). He denounces the illegitimate worship practices of the Judeans (44:8) and says that the "remnant" in Egypt will be a dead end; they will never be part of Judah again (44:14). The people are obstinate to the very end, however, and evidently conclude that ceasing worship of other gods, particularly the queen of heaven, was the start of their troubles (44:17-18). The women declare that they will continue making their offerings, to which Jeremiah replies, "By all means, keep your vows and make your libations!" and "All the people of Judah who are in the land of Egypt shall perish by the sword and by famine, until not one is left" (44:25, 27). Jeremiah's attitude toward the Judean refugees to Egypt is the exact opposite of how he views the Babylonian exiles, the "good figs" of chapter 24.

Jeremiah 46–52

The final section of Jeremiah comprises a series of "oracles against the nations," including several smaller states near Judah as well as Egypt and Babylon. These oracles are similar in structure and theology to other oracles of this type we have seen. What makes these prophecies distinct is how they incorporate Jeremiah's perspective on the end of the Judean state. Regional nations such as Moab and Ammon have survived intact so far, but Jeremiah promises that they will receive just as much judgment as Judah and pay for their arrogance and smug attitude. Similarly, Babylon has been used by God as a tool of punishment, but it will not escape divine judgment for its own wickedness.

Chapter 46 contains an oracle predicting Babylonian conquest of Egypt. It begins with the battle of Carchemish in 605, the end of any effective Assyrian and Egyptian resistance to the rise of Babylon (46:1-6). The Egyptians have sought to rise and cover the earth like a flooding Nile (46:7-8), but the Lord will attack with a "sword that shall devour and be sated, and drink its fill of their blood" (46:10).

The next three chapters cover a series of smaller nations, close but with generally increasing distance from Judah: Philistia (47), Moab (48), Ammon (49:1-6), Edom (49:7-22),

Aram (49:23-27), Kedar (49:28-33), and Elam (49:34-39). These oracles draw upon a series of creative metaphors for God's judgment, each of which is connected in some way to the identity of the recipient. Each of these nations is guilty and deserves to be punished by the Lord of history, although the text does not always specify what their sins might be. Some of the descriptions are shocking in their violence, but even if the sword of the Lord causes great destruction, the prophet asks, "How can it be quiet, when the LORD has given it an order?" (47:7).

Moab's sin was its arrogance and security while Israel was being attacked (48:29-30). The nation is said to have "trusted in [its] strongholds and your treasures," living in quiet safety while others suffered. Verse 11 compares Moab to a jar of wine that sat undisturbed and flavorful but that God will now "decant him, and empty his vessels, and break his jars into pieces." Moab had been seen as "mighty" and "glorious" (48:17) but now will have its arm broken (i.e., its power, 48:25). Moab had "magnified itself against the LORD" but now will "wallow in his vomit" and be a "laughingstock" after it laughed at Israel (48:26; cf. 48:42).

The Ammonites are guilty of taking land that had belonged to the Israelite tribe of Gad and will now have their land dispossessed by Israel (49:1-2). This complaint recalls the words of Amos against Ammon, that they have "ripped open pregnant women in Gilead in order to enlarge their territory" (Amos 1:13). Jeremiah had declared that the Moabite god Chemosh would "go out into exile" with his priests (48:7), and now he says that the Ammonite god Milcom "shall go into exile" with the people (49:3). This reference to gods going into exile reflects the Mesopotamian practice of capturing god statues and taking them physically back to the capital city. Such relocation of the statue is a physical marker for the god's defeat by Marduk or, indirectly in this case, the Lord.

In the oracle against Edom, the prophet mentions "the cup" that the nations are required to drink, a reference to the cup of wrath that Jeremiah (symbolically) makes all the nations drink in 25:15-26 (cf. Babylon as the cup of God's

God's Servants, the Prophets

wrath in 51:7). If innocent people are caught up in the warfare and suffer ("drink from the cup"), then those who are guilty certainly cannot avoid it. In this case, however, the innocent widows and orphans of Edom can trust in God's protection (49:11). Interestingly, three of the nations receive a final positive promise that their fortunes will be restored "in the latter days": Moab (48:47), Ammon (49:6), and Elam (49:39).

Chapters 50–51 present a long and complicated reflection on the nation of Babylon, whose imperial power has loomed like a shadow over the whole book and, to some extent, over the whole of the preexilic prophetic tradition. These oracles seem to date from the latter period of the exile, perhaps to about the same time as the prophecies of Second Isaiah in the mid-sixth century BCE. Given the fact that God has used Babylon for divine purposes of judgment, what now? Similar questions have already been raised by Isaiah (10:5-17) and Habakkuk (1:5-17), and they get to the heart of God's justice and lordship. Will such a vicious nation receive justice for its crimes, and can Israel hope for salvation from their hand?

Jeremiah says that a people from the north will attack Babylon (50:2-3, 41-43; 51:11), ironic since they were the people from the north who attacked Israel (1:13-15). The perspective on Babylon has changed dramatically in this oracle. Israel has been scattered because its shepherds were incompetent (50:6) and its enemies have considered themselves innocent because God was judging Israel (50:7). But now those who have plundered will find themselves plundered (50:10), the "hammer of the earth" now cut down and broken (50:23; cf. 51:20-23). The "arrogant one shall stumble and fall" (50:32), once again recalling the arrogant boasting of the king of Assyria in Isaiah 10.

Chapter 51 initially turns toward lamentation. The Judeans living in Babylon are told to run for their lives (51:6, 45), to wail for the slain men of the city (50:8), and finally to return home to Zion in vindication (50:10, 50). Verses 34-35 contain a quotation from the city of Jerusalem, which has been devoured and crushed by Babylon and now calls on God to avenge its "torn flesh" on Babylon. Such a sentiment is not far from the calls for vindication in the book of Lamentations. However, in this case God provides the answer that never arrives in that book: "I am going to defend your cause and take vengeance for you" (51:36).

The final chapter of Jeremiah incorporates material from chapter 39 on the final siege of Jerusalem by Nebuchadnezzar and from 2 Kings 25:27-30 on the hopeful situation of King Jehoiachin in exile. In between there is a description of the city's breach, the burning of the temple, and the confiscation and destruction of the temple furnishings and architecture. This bleak narrative sets the stage for the book that follows next in the Old Testament canon, the book of Lamentations.

Lamentations

The book of Lamentations contains five poems of "lament" over the destruction of Jerusalem by the Babylonians in 586 BCE. The text follows the book of Jeremiah in the Christian Old Testament, with the implicit suggestion that Jeremiah is the author of the book. This association derives from the Septuagint, the Greek translation of the Hebrew Bible begun in the third century BCE, which placed Lamentations after Jeremiah and included an ascription saying that "Jeremiah sat weeping and composed this lament over Jerusalem." Certainly Jeremiah is the most emotive of the Hebrew prophets, and Jeremiah 9:1 gives rise to the identification of Jeremiah as a "weeping prophet." However, nothing in the book itself suggests that Jeremiah is the author, and it is included among the "Writings" in the Hebrew canon rather than with the prophets.

The five poems present different perspectives on the fall of the city, including those of an outside observer, of the city itself, and of those who suffer in its midst. The first four chapters each follow an "acrostic" pattern in which each stanza begins with a specific letter of the Hebrew alphabet, beginning with *aleph* and continuing through *bet* and so on. The purpose of this form is unclear, though it may have aided in memorization or public recitation of the poetry. The acrostic form is well attested in the ancient world, as is the "lament for a fallen city" genre itself. Sumerian laments for the destruction of Ur, Sumer, Nippur, etc., date from the second millennium BCE.

The first chapter draws upon prophetic comparisons of Jerusalem to a female, in this case a widow forsaken by her lovers and friends. Her precious and private possessions have been pawed over by her enemies (1:10), and her festivals have given way to famine. In v. 11 the poem switches from the perspective of an observer to that of the city itself, speaking in the first person. She calls out to God for relief, emphasizing her distress and anguish at being "trodden as in a wine press" by God. As often happens in lament psalms, the personified city finally asks for God to bring judgment on those who are glad at her trouble, saying, "Deal with them as you have dealt with me" (1:22; cf. 3:64-66).

The central cause of the city's distress is God's punishment for their sins, and several verses recognize the justice of their suffering (1:8, 18; 3:42; 4:11). However, the text also raises several issues that call God's actions into question. It points out that their punishment has been exceptionally severe (4:6) and asks whether it has been unjustly applied to the descendants of guilty ancestors (5:7). How guilty could the children be? However, they bear a disproportionate share of the city's suffering (1:16; 2:19), with infants fainting from hunger in the streets (2:11-12). How could the people have been expected to know better when their prophets have delivered to them "false and deceptive visions" (2:14)? Chapter 3 includes a section of confident affirmation of God's mercy (3:22-33), saying that God "does not willingly afflict or grieve anyone" (3:33). When terrible things happen, "does the LORD not see it?" (3:36). This pious expression of God's justice, however, is called into question by the depth of Jerusalem's pain resulting from God "killing without pity" (3:43).

The poetry compares God to any number of impersonal and destructive forces of nature. God has burned like a flaming fire, raging in destructive acts of violence against Israel (2:2-3), and like a bear or a lion sitting in ambush (3:10). God has become "like an enemy" (2:5) and has driven the city into darkness; "against me alone he turns his hand, again and again, all day long" (3:3). Theologically, the poems walk a fine line between affirming the justice of God's punishment and the harsh possibility of God's caprice or overreaction in sending judgment.

Either way, the description of the city's suffering is brutally intense. Even if the people deserve wrath, their attackers are violent, wicked, and filled with mocking for God's people (3:61). They experience great famine (1:11), even to the point where it is a form of compassion for a mother to cook and eat her own children (2:20).

The rhetorical purpose of this kind of lamentation is twofold: to provide a cathartic communal expression of grief and frustration and to ask God for assistance. As with lament psalms, the people hope that this intense description of pain and suffering will motivate God to show compassion and deliver them from their distress. At the same time, the people also confess their trust in God's goodness and power, which serves the same two purposes (3:22-24). If God is powerful enough to save and good enough to care deeply for the people, then God is their best and only hope.

The last stanza of Lamentations combines an affirmation of God's sovereignty ("you, O LORD, reign forever," 5:19) with an honest questioning ("Why have you forgotten us completely?" 5:20). The people hope that God will restore the city to its former greatness, but even in faith there remains a seed of doubt in the last line: "unless you have utterly rejected us, and are angry with us beyond measure" (5:22). In their distress, God's final absence is a terrifying possibility, yet they still address God in prayer, expressing not so much hope as a desperate need for divine salvation.

Chapter 9

Obadiah

Introduction

Barely taking up one page in the Bible, the book of Obadiah is known more as part of a hastily memorized list of the minor prophets than for its content. The prophet predicts the destruction of Edom at the hands of the Babylonians. There is no dating formula, and the prophecies mention a wide range of historical events, but internal evidence suggests that Obadiah wrote sometime between the Babylonian attacks on Jerusalem in 597 BCE and the time of Edom's fall around 550 BCE. It is associated in the tradition with Jeremiah since both prophets reflect upon the larger repercussions of the destruction of Jerusalem in 586 BCE. Lamentations also blames Edom for their part in the fall of Jerusalem (4:21-22). Interestingly, Obadiah does not attribute the foreign attacks on Israel and Judah to God's divine punishment. Rather, he sees these events as the tragic outcome of foreign aggression, aided and abetted by the gleeful Edomites. In Obadiah's view, Edom will pay for that treachery in due course.

Historical Context

Genesis 25–28 and 32 trace the ancestry of Edom to Esau, the brother of Jacob. These Genesis narratives do not explain the actual origins of Edom as much as reflect the tense relationship between the kingdoms of Israel and Judah with the southeastern neighbor. Edom is singled out for prophetic denunciation in Amos 1, Isaiah 34, Jeremiah 49, and several places in Ezekiel, not to mention Balaam's prediction of Edom's doom in Numbers 24:18. Amos says that Edom "pursued his brother with the sword," presumably meaning Israel (1:11). The series of oracles in Amos describes a complex scene of tense regional conflicts involving Israel and neighboring countries like Edom and Moab during the early eighth century BCE. Writing during the Babylonian exile, Ezekiel says that Edom "acted revengefully against the house of Judah" (25:12), "rejoiced over the house of Israel, because it was desolate" (35:15), and "with wholehearted joy and utter contempt, took my land as their possession" (36:5).

The biblical picture of Edom's acrimonious relationship with Israel and Judah is supported by extrabiblical evidence. We know from Assyrian annals that Edom paid tribute to Tiglath-Pileser III along with the other regional nations. A fragmentary Judean text from Arad suggests that Edom refused to participate in Hezekiah's rebellion against Sennacherib in 701 BCE, and the records of Ashurbanipal suggest that Edom contributed soldiers to his campaign against Egypt in the early seventh century BCE. Archaeological investigation has also shown Edomite presence in the Negeb in the seventh and sixth centuries BCE. Although there is no evidence outside the Bible that Edom participated in the Babylonian sack of Jerusalem, Edom certainly did not participate in the Judean rebellion of 587 BCE. Judean survivors of this catastrophe placed some share of blame on Edom, a nation that was itself destroyed by Babylonian King Nabonidus in 550 BCE.

Theological Traditions

Like most of the prophetic books, the central theological questions being addressed in Obadiah involve the nature of divine justice, God's role as Lord of history, and the possibility of a restored community returned to its land with a renewed identity. Obadiah affirms that God has the power and motivation

Obadiah

to establish justice in the world by punishing the Edomites for their acts of violence against Israel and Judah. Contributing to the seriousness of their crimes is the traditional understanding in the Bible that Israel and Edom descend from the brothers Jacob and Esau.

In Obadiah we also see the beginnings of a terminological and theological shift in Judean national identity that intensifies during and after the Babylonian exile. Following the early reigns of Saul, David, and Solomon, the united monarchy divided into the northern kingdom of Israel and the southern kingdom of Judah. After Israel's destruction in 722 BCE, Judah continued to be known as Judah, with a memory of lost Israel. In the late seventh century the expansionist policies of Josiah seemed to envision a restored and reunited Israel. When Judah was in exile, they increasingly saw themselves as the righteous remnant of *Israel* in a larger theological sense, not just of the kingdom of Judah. Obadiah sometimes uses the terms "Jacob," "Joseph," and "Israel," all terms that mean "northern kingdom of Israel" in the eighth-century prophets, along with "Zion" and "Jerusalem," which generally mean "the southern kingdom of Judah." However, notice that in vv. 17-21, Obadiah equates these terms to imply a newly reformed kingdom of Israel ruled from Jerusalem. He says that the Judean and Israelite remnant will possess the lands even beyond Israel that were formerly under David's dominion (vv. 19-20).

As we move into the exilic and postexilic periods, this vision of universal restoration will become more prominent. The developing theological idea is that when God restores Judah from its Babylonian captivity, that will mean the rebirth of Israel. With the absence of political autonomy, Judah reclaims the mantle of Israelite identity.

Literary Features

From a literary perspective the book is less daunting. A slightly revised version of vv. 1-4 is found in Jeremiah 49:14-16, which gives us a glimpse into the literary processes that may lie behind the production of prophetic books. The textual history of prophetic books can be complicated. Smaller texts were collected and edited together. Though the final form of each book may bear the name of a particular prophet, those names are more a shorthand for the collection than a claim that all the texts were actually spoken by the "original" prophet. It may be that Obadiah's oracle existed in a shorter form that was incorporated into Jeremiah or that the editors of Jeremiah intentionally quoted and revised just this part of Obadiah. In either case it is a good reminder to see the prophetic books as the product of a long traditioning process rather than the sayings of a single person.

Some of the earlier prophetic motifs that show up here are the use of a messenger report (v. 1), comparison with a hypothetical situation (v. 5), and references to the day of the Lord (vv. 8, 15). Notable as well are highly formulaic repetitions in vv. 12-14 and 19-21. Each of these introduces a series of actions that form a short, powerful litany of offenses (12-14) or their effects (19-21).

Commentary

Consisting of only twenty-one verses, Obadiah is essentially one judgment oracle against the nation of Edom. A report has come that Edom is under attack, and the prophet predicts total defeat and humiliation for Judah's longtime enemy. The descriptions of Edom's arrogance and of its fall are fairly standard prophetic rhetoric. Edom has boasted proudly that no one will be able to bring them down, much like the arrogant boasting of the king of Assyria (Isa 10:5) and the king of Babylon (Isa 14:12-20). God's ability to reach even into the heights of the heavens for judgment is expressed most powerfully in Amos 9:2-4, which is itself a reversal of Psalm 139:7-12, in which the psalmist wonders, "Where can I flee from your presence?"

Edom will be pillaged and attacked by its former allies and co-conspirators (v. 7). The reason for this punishment is that Edom stood idly by, and even participated, as Israel and Judah were plundered and defeated by foreign enemies. Rather than coming to the aid of their "brother," a reference to the filial bond between Jacob and Esau in Genesis 25–28, the Edomites gloated (v. 12), came into Jerusalem to participate in the looting (v. 13), and handed over escaping Judeans to the Babylonians (v. 14).

Thus, this exilic or perhaps late preexilic prophecy looks back at the last 150 years of the Israelite and Judean nations and sees divine justice in the coming destruction of Edom at the hands of the Babylonian invaders. The prophet says, "As you have done, it shall be done to you" (v. 15). After Edom has been broken and "gulped down" by foreign invaders, the remnant of Israel and Judah shall take control of the Edomite territory.

The prophet ends with a vision of Israelite restoration that mirrors the time of David. Obadiah does not specifically mention the united monarchy, though he says in vv. 19-20 that the Judean remnant will possess the traditional lands of Israel (Shephelah, Ephraim, Samaria, Benjamin, and Gilead) and that their control also will extend northward into Phoenicia, southward into the Negeb, and eastward over Edom. This does not reflect the total extent of David's empire, but it is certainly an ambitious vision for the sixth century BCE.

Finally, although Obadiah foresees the restoration of Israel and Jerusalem, he says nothing in particular about a king or royal messiah. The closest that we have is the reference to "the house of Jacob" and "the house of Joseph" that sets fire to "the house of Esau" in v. 18. The "survivors" of Israel and Judah possess the lands that come under their control; it is not a matter of the royal line reasserting hegemony over ancient territories. The righteous remnant march from Jerusalem to "rule Mount Esau." Thus, Obadiah should be interpreted alongside the possibly exilic texts of Zephaniah 3:15 and Micah 7:14, which place Judah's hope not in a human king but in the direct rule of God from Zion.

Chapter 10

Conclusion

Introduction

Different interpretations of the Bible arise when people have different assumptions about what the Bible is, when they do not share the same goals for their interpretation, and when they are situated within divergent reading communities. Those who find themselves in an argument about the Bible should take a moment to analyze how their different assumptions, goals, and contexts have led them to that point.

In this concluding chapter, we will look briefly at four issues that tend to create controversy and division among readers of the Bible: 1) the relationship between history and theology in the Bible, 2) the place of the prophets in the Old Testament, 3) the connection between the prophets and the New Testament, and 4) the relevance of the prophets today. Each of these topics could fill a book of its own, so we will only begin to explore the many issues involved. The argument in this chapter is that different ways of interpreting the prophets each have their merits. There is no single "right" way to read the Bible, but a "good" reading is one that is clear about its suppositions and goals and one that lets itself be guided primarily by the text rather than by an external agenda.

History and Theology

We have focused our attention on the prophetic literary tradition rather than trying to reconstruct a personal biography for each prophet. Within this literary study, however, our interpretation has revolved around the central issues of history and theology. Even though we cannot know all we would prefer to know about the history of the prophets, we must begin our interpretation by situating the text within its historical context. This historical approach to interpretation will help avoid the temptation to hear the prophets as disembodied voices with no basis for careful interpretation. The historical context of the prophetic literature is an essential starting point that sets the stage for our reading, even though our interpretation will not end there. Even if we are interested more in theology than history, the theological ideas in the prophetic text are themselves influenced by historical events, with each prophet applying those ideas to his own context. Interpretation of the Bible must take into account its historical context and development over time.

By way of summary, here are four key affirmations about the relationship between history and theology in prophetic interpretation.

1. Theological ideas in the prophets emerge out of their historical context, which is the essential starting point for interpretation.
2. The history of Israel and Judah is long and complex, which helps explain why there is similar theological development in the prophetic tradition.
3. Although political and social factors are important aspects of their historical context, we should not reduce the prophets to such material concerns. The prophets talk about the world in which they live, but they also make authentic theological claims about God.
4. Already within the prophets we have evidence for the creative reuse and reinterpretation of prophetic ideas. Historical context provides a controlled starting point for

Conclusion

interpretation, but the original context becomes one aspect of our dynamic engagement with prophetic theology.

These points affirm the importance of both historical and theological modes of interpretation and argue that a good and faithful reading of the prophets will hold these two modes in creative tension. Slipping too far into the historical mode may cause one to dismiss the prophets as merely historical actors when in fact their role as historical actors is the key to their identity as God's chosen servants. Slipping too far into the theological mode may cause one to read the prophets selfishly or arrogantly, assuming that the prophetic word speaks only or primarily to us and our concerns. The critical distance created by the historical context reminds us to be careful and respectful readers.

These four affirmations are the basis for the next three sections. How should we interpret the prophets within the larger Old Testament tradition, in connection with the New Testament, or within our own world? We should begin by holding historical and theological dimensions in creative tension, always considering the historical process behind the Bible's development and canonization.

Before continuing, we will take a brief look at a passage that captures well the creative tension between history and theology, Amos 9:1-6, one of the many texts that predicts God's violent destruction of Israel. What sense are we to make of a text in which God personally destroys every living member of the Israelite community? Amos 9:4 says, "Though they go into captivity in front of their enemies, there I will command the sword, and it shall kill them; and I will fix my eyes on them for harm and not for good."

It is obvious that this text poses serious challenges for a theological reading of Scripture. How can this text be said to describe the God whom Jews and Christians worship? Is God filled with hatred and bloodlust? Does this text simply express God's righteous judgment, a view held by some contemporary Christians who conclude from this passage that God's wrath is pure and just and that a people justly condemned has no right to complain about their punishment? This theology of retribution is sometimes employed to make sense of tragedies such as terrorist attacks and hurricanes, although many of us instinctively reject this view of God's sovereignty. By considering the interaction of history and theology in this text, we can at least begin to make some sense of it.

First, we must ask *why* Amos uses such harsh language. Prophetic theology is always prophetic rhetoric. In other words, the prophets make theological statements not for the purpose of objective or dispassionate description, but rather as arguments intended for listeners who are situated in their time and place. Amos, speaking to a people "who feel secure on Mount Samaria" (6:1), must make his argument as extreme and shocking as possible. Objectively speaking, did God truly plan to kill every last one of them? I would say no, and in fact they did not all die. However, from a rhetorical point of view, it is clear that Amos wants them to consider that possibility strongly. The people need to make changes and are not in a position to "hear" a more moderate message.

Second, Amos's imagery draws upon a larger theological and rhetorical tradition. In our discussion of Amos 9, we pointed out that this oracle reverses the affirmation of God's reach in Psalm 139:7, in which the psalmist prays, "Where can I flee from your presence?" Amos does not invent the idea of God's unlimited presence; he employs imagery and theology that is known to his audience. In addition, Amos's prophecies have a profound impact on later prophetic rhetoric. This early passage helps us recognize the ongoing conversation about why God would send destruction on Israel and Judah. What we soon realize is that this theology of retribution, as harsh as it may be, is only part of a larger narrative of God's redemption and mercy. Even though judgment is (nearly) the end of the story in Amos, it is not the end of the story in the prophets. Even staying within the prophetic tradition, we can place the judgment of God within a larger theology of God's grace and redemption. We can examine the relationships between different prophetic texts without losing any particular voice in the shuffle.

Third, it would be a mistake to simply write this passage off as a limited text bound by its own time. God's violent retribution is not found only here, but is a central theological problem in all the prophets, indeed the whole Bible. Even though we cannot accept the metaphor of God as violent killer, we should not simply ignore these prophetic texts for two reasons. First, if we are to engage the Bible as a whole, we cannot only read the parts that are easy. Second, some people are inclined to use a text like this in an uncritical and damaging way, and ignoring the problem will not help us confront such problematic interpretation. This troubling text from Amos was an authentic theological expression within its own context, and a "good" interpretation of it in our own context must be subtle and tentative. Amos 9 is part of a larger tradition with which we engage and a reminder that extreme violent rhetoric is not new and is not the final word.

The Prophets and the Old Testament

In this section we will consider the relationship between the prophets and other sections of the Hebrew Bible, including the Torah, the historical narratives, and the Wisdom literature. Since the Bible is more like a library than a book, there is no single "Old Testament theology" found in every part of the canon. Rather, the Old Testament is more like an intense panel discussion or a long conference in which various panelists and audience members engage the conversation at different times. The Bible's central affirmation is that God is Lord, but its coherence comes more from its questions than from its answers. The Bible engages the complex realities of the world, but biblical authors engage these complexities in different ways. It is not surprising to find similarities and differences between the prophets and other parts of the Bible. As part of a larger interpretive process, these canonical relationships are complex and rich.

We will briefly discuss these issues using the ordering of the Jewish canon. The Jewish Bible is called the "Tanakh," which is an acronym for the three parts of the canon, the

Torah, Nebi'im, and Ketubim (that is, the "Law," the "Prophets," and the "Writings"). The Torah contains the first five books of the Bible. The Nebi'im comprises the Deuteronomistic History (Joshua, Judges, Samuel, and Kings) as well as the writing prophets. Finally, the Ketubim is everything else, including the Wisdom literature, Psalms, and other historical and folk narratives.

To begin with the Torah, the prophets draw implicitly upon the covenantal traditions found in Genesis through Deuteronomy, but they tend to emphasize ethical behavior more than ritual observance. Since the prophets sometimes offer a critique of ritual activity like sacrifice, some interpreters have concluded that the prophets actually reject the ritual traditions of the Torah. For example, in the late nineteenth century, Julius Wellhausen popularized the "source-critical approach" to the development of the Torah. Wellhausen's goal was to use the textual layers of the biblical text as a window into the development of Israelite religion. In other words, he assumed that as the worship and theology of Israel changed over time, those changes would be revealed by a comparison of early and later documents. Wellhausen identified four strands within the Torah and argued that the final layer was the work of a priestly writer who was responsible for the ritual and legal material in Exodus, Leviticus, and Numbers. Wellhausen argued that this priestly ritual derived from the last stage of Jewish religion, a temple cult dominated by external rules and rigid legalism. He argued that the prophets represent an older and more authentically spiritual version of Israelite religion.

What is clear in hindsight is that Wellhausen was influenced by his own preference for free and dynamic "spiritual" religion over "empty" ritualism. Wellhausen, like many from the Protestant West, preferred the spiritual purity of the prophets to the ritual legalism of the Torah. When the prophets critique Israel's ritual worship, therefore, interpreters like Wellhausen conclude that there is an essential contrast between ritual and emotional worship, between sacrifice and ethical action, between priests and prophets.

Conclusion

There are two problems with this contrast between the Torah and the prophets. First, priestly ritual in the Torah already incorporates an ethical and spiritual standard that is very "prophetic." For example, the concept of "holiness" is used to encourage social justice in Leviticus 17–26, and one's confession of sin is the key aspect of the purification offering in Leviticus 5:5. There is nothing mechanical or automatic about priestly ritual. Second, the prophets suggest that God has rejected the people's worship not because it is *ritual* but because the people are sinful and have no right to address God in worship. In Amos 5:22 God says, "Even though you offer me your burnt offerings and grain offerings, I will not accept them," and in Isaiah 58:6 God says, "Is not this the fast that I choose: to loose the bonds of injustice?" The prophets are not arguing that religion should not have a ritual component. To the contrary, there are many positive references to ritual activity in the prophets. The prophets believe, however, that ritual worship should take place within the context of a relationship with God based on integrity and justice. In this ethical conviction, they agree with the priestly writers completely.

The second major canonical section to consider comprises the historical books of the "former prophets," Joshua, Judges, Samuel, and Kings. These books are included among the Nebi'im (the "Prophets") for two reasons. First, the historical narrative tells the story of many prophetic characters, including the key figures of Samuel, Nathan, Elijah, Elisha, and the prophetess Huldah. These historical narratives help us understand the social context for the oracles found in the written prophetic books. Some figures were "central prophets" with recognized administrative authority and access to the halls of power. This seems to be the case for Isaiah and Jeremiah. Historical narratives about central prophets like Nathan and Micaiah ben Imlah illustrate the complexities of that sociopolitical situation (2 Sam 12; 1 Kgs 22). Other figures were "peripheral prophets" who preached the word of God from an outsider's perspective. Wanderers like Amos have religious authority by virtue of their calling as prophets, but they do not serve any official political role. In the historical narratives we see this type of peripheral activity in the ministry of Elijah (cf. 1 Kgs 18–29) and in the work of a nameless prophet identified only as "a man of God," who in fact may have been Amos (1 Kgs 13).

It is also true that the historical narratives themselves reflect a prophetic outlook on the world. As the story of Israel unfolds, the historians affirm that God is the Lord of history who directs the affairs of Israel, Judah, and other nations in order to fulfill divine purposes. Kings are held accountable for their ethical lapses, for their promotion of injustice, and for their religious transgressions. After David, only two kings receive generally positive evaluation from the historical writer Hezekiah (2 Kgs 18:3) and Josiah (2 Kgs 23:25); all others are presented as flawed, weak, or totally corrupt. That same message is found in almost every prophetic book and plays a central role in their understanding of Israel's present and future.

Finally, the third major section of the Hebrew Bible is the Ketubim, the "Writings." These include the Psalms, Wisdom literature, additional historical material in Ezra–Chronicles, and narratives such as Ruth, Esther, and Daniel. We have seen that the prophets draw upon genres associated primarily with these books. For example, both Habakkuk's "lament" (Hab 1:1–4) and his "praise hymn" (Hab 3) are similar to material found in the Psalms. In particular, the prophets use motifs found in the Wisdom literature (Proverbs, Ecclesiastes, Job). Some scholars have suggested that the prophets and Wisdom literature are radically different, but the stronger argument is that the prophets sometimes draw upon Wisdom genres to communicate their message. For example, in the "Song of the Vineyard" in Isaiah 5, the prophet uses an allegorical technique common to Wisdom literature, and Jeremiah quotes a parable in Jeremiah 31:29. The prophets are not sages, but they address a people who are familiar with folktales, songs, and Wisdom sayings and use these forms to their rhetorical advantage.

In comparing the theology of the prophets to that of the Wisdom literature, the most important issue is how these

Conclusion

writers understand the justice of God in a world of suffering. As we have seen, the prophets draw on the covenantal tradition to explain phenomena like invasion, drought, and illness in terms of divine punishment for sin. In general, the scope of their interpretation is broad. They are interested primarily in larger political and social movements and how these reveal the working of God's justice, both in wrath and mercy.

The Wisdom literature is different in two important ways. The Wisdom books in the Bible have a scope that is more individual than communal. Proverbs and Ecclesiastes are "practical" Wisdom books while Job is more philosophical, but each of these is interested primarily in how individuals should understand the workings of the world and find their own way in the midst of it. The book of Proverbs includes advice for how a person should follow the way of God to find success, happiness, and long life. Ecclesiastes and Job raise questions about the reliability of such a system in guaranteeing health and happiness, but their scope is still mostly at the individual level. Job does raise its focus to the cosmic level, reflecting on the nature of creation itself, but the question in Job 38–42 is whether an individual has any standing before God in this vast and unpredictable universe.

The second major difference is not as stark. The Wisdom literature allows more room for a skeptical perspective on the nature of suffering in the world. Although Proverbs is highly optimistic about our ability to understand the world and be successful in it, Ecclesiastes and Job raise the possibility that the world may not make sense. Job is angry because he believes that God has wrongly inflicted suffering on him. In Job 9–10, for example, Job suggests that God is a tyrant, a powerful ruler who wields power in a manner that is insensitive to its effects on the world. The ending of Job affirms God's power and sovereignty but does not neatly resolve Job's dilemma. This view of God is quite different from the rational and just God of the prophets, who directs all events according to divine purposes. Ecclesiastes agrees with Job that the world does not always make sense and that good things perish while wicked things prosper. The Teacher is not angry like Job but rather counsels a spirit of moderation and detachment, suggesting that people will be happiest when they find their way as best they can in a world of uncertainty.

The prophets' entire reason for prophesying is to mitigate any uncertainty or doubt about what will happen and why. For example, in Isaiah 58 the people question God, asking, "Why do we fast, but you do not see?" (v. 3). Such a question would be at home in Job as well as in the lament tradition of the Psalms. In this case, however, the prophet provides the answer: "Look, you serve your own interests on your fast day, and oppress all your workers." In the prophetic tradition, suffering is not a mystery. Such difficulties are either the result of God's just punishment or possibly a temporary situation into which God is about to intervene for their salvation. Of course, some prophets are more plaintive than others, in particular Habakkuk and Jeremiah. The lament of Habakkuk (1:1-5) is more understandable when read in light of the larger canon of the Old Testament.

The Prophets and the New Testament

The relationship between the Old Testament and the New Testament is a large and complicated issue in biblical interpretation and in the history of Christian theology. In order to understand this issue, one must know what the "Old Testament" and the "New Testament" actually are. The Old Testament is also known as the Hebrew Bible, and it forms the basis of the Jewish scriptures. The Old Testament is a complex library of traditions with a centuries-long history.

In the third century BCE Jews began to translate the Hebrew Bible into the common language of the time, Greek. This Greek version of the Hebrew Bible is called the Septuagint, and it was read alongside other Jewish works that were written during the last three or four centuries BCE, texts that are collectively known as the Apocrypha or the Deuterocanonical books. Most scholars believe that the New Testament writers read and quoted from the Septuagint rather

Conclusion

than the Hebrew Bible, and there is evidence as well that they were familiar with the Apocrypha.

The history of Judaism during these centuries is also complex. Jews lived under Persian domination, then Greek domination, and finally Roman domination. They continued to disperse throughout the world, and they developed a variety of responses to the imperial world in which they lived. Some Jews cooperated with the Greek and Roman authorities while others participated in insurrections and opposition movements. The textual, theology, and political history of Judaism was such that by the first century CE, there was great diversity within Judaism, including a vibrant reformist and prophetic tradition.

It is this prophetic, even apocalyptic tradition that is home to John the Baptist and to the man he baptizes, Jesus of Nazareth. The "historical Jesus" is elusive, but when we read the Gospels, we must conclude that Jesus was deeply influenced by the Hebrew prophetic and apocalyptic traditions. In Luke 4, Jesus reads from the scriptures as part of the inauguration of his ministry. The text is Isaiah 61:1: "The Spirit of the Lord is upon me, because he has anointed me to bring good news to the poor. He has sent me to proclaim release to the captives and recovery of sight to the blind, to let the oppressed go free, to proclaim the year of the Lord's favor."

There are many theological and literary implications of Jesus' quotation of this passage, but it is clear that Jesus sees himself as part of the larger prophetic tradition. And even more, he concludes by saying to his listeners that "today this scripture has been fulfilled in your hearing" (Luke 4:21). The interpretation and application of the prophetic literature continued into later Christian preaching about Jesus and eventually made its way into the Gospels. Often, New Testament writers cite prophetic passages that Jesus "fulfills" in his teachings, miracles, death, and resurrection. This theological connection between the prophets and the New Testament is intricate and important.

In summary, Jesus' ministry was rooted in the prophetic tradition, and the New Testament writers quote the prophets to support their presentation of Jesus as the Messiah. What, if anything, does this mean for one's reading of the prophets themselves? Should the New Testament's use of the prophets influence the way that one reads the prophetic text itself? Is a "Christological" approach helpful or appropriate for reading the Old Testament?

First, the answer depends on the *reading community* in which this interpretation takes place. In a Jewish context, for example, a Christological interpretation is not appropriate. It would be tempting for Christians to look at Jewish interpretation from the outside and view it as defective or incomplete. However, one must appreciate the complex history of Judaism that led up to the beginning of the Christian movement in the first century CE. The Christian interpretation of the Messiah and of the Suffering Servant was not the *only* way that these texts were read at the time, or since. In fact, Paul says that the "crucified messiah" is "a stumbling block to Jews" (1 Cor 1:23). Christian interpretation of the prophets was not obvious then (nor is it now), and the Jews had (and have) their own interpretive traditions that developed in different ways. It would be helpful for Christian readers to spend more effort understanding how Jews interpret the Bible, and why. Jewish interpretation has coherence and validity within their community, and it may have much to teach those outside the tradition.

Within the Christian community, however, a Christological reading is appropriate. Christians believe that the God who called and promised to redeem Israel in the prophets is the same God who is the father of Jesus Christ, the God who inspired both the prophets and Paul. Therefore, Christians affirm the essential theological unity of the whole Bible, Old Testament and New Testament.

The issue is not as simple as this affirmation, however. The second issue is the *goal* of the interpretation. Regardless of one's religious community, readers should begin their interpretation by attending to historical questions. If the goal of the interpretation is historical, then an overarching Christological hermeneutic might obscure the text more than it illuminates.

Conclusion

The most familiar example of this is the text we discussed in Isaiah, the prophecy that "a virgin shall conceive" (7:14). Even though this verse is quoted in Matthew 1:23, that text's primary meaning is rooted in the Assyrian crisis of the late eighth century BCE. Jewish, Christian, and non-religious readers should be able to agree on the historical methods used to explore this passage and discuss their conclusions on an even basis.

If the goal of the interpretation is theological, then perhaps a larger Christological hermeneutic may be appropriate, but this is where people begin to disagree about their interpretations. The more rooted in a specific theological tradition one's interpretation may be, the less it will be accessible to an outside reader. Even so, it is possible to discuss biblical theology from a historical point of view, considering how ideas grew and developed over time. Different interpreters should be able to agree about the general trajectory of biblical theology even if they identify more with one particular part of the tradition. For example, it is appropriate within a Christian community to read the Suffering Servant passages in Isaiah as messianic prophecies of Christ's suffering and death. From a historical point of view, however, we know that the Servant Songs were not interpreted by Jews as messianic. Jews and Christians took this motif of righteous suffering in different directions, and a historical approach to biblical theology helps us understand those developments.

The notion of "trajectories" can be a helpful concept. Jewish and Christian theology developed through parallel and increasingly divergent trajectories. By the time we get to the first century CE, there were several different Jewish trajectories. The nascent Christian movement, initially a reform movement within Judaism, was a part of this world of Jewish biblical interpretation. It became a religion in its own right by the end of the first century CE, but Christianity continued to fragment and change over time. It was not until the fourth century CE that the Constantinian church hierarchy began to establish a Christian "orthodoxy" that set "correct" boundaries for biblical interpretation. Since the Reformation of the sixteenth century, the Christian community has continued to fracture along theological and ecclesiological lines.

The purpose of recognizing these different trajectories within Jewish and Christian history is to remind ourselves that each person's theological interpretation of the Bible is contextual. We are each the heirs of our own tradition. That does not mean that every reading is equal or that nothing is really "true." However, it does mean that each individual should exercise honesty and humility in how they approach the theological interpretation of others. Such engagement can be mutually enlightening and community building.

An awareness of the Bible's historical context does not rule out the highest goal of biblical interpretation: proclamation. When Matthew quotes Isaiah, he is not making a historical argument or even reflecting on the history of messianic theology. He is making a theological claim on his readers, inviting them to respond to the story of Jesus with faith and obedience. A historical reading of the Bible does not rule out this kind of proclamation, but neither does faith in Christ as the Messiah eliminate the need for careful, historical exegesis of the Old Testament.

One way to express the argument in this section is to envision the reading of the Bible in two directions. One direction is historical, encountering each text in its historical context from the past to the present. In a *forward* reading, the historical context of each prophecy is primary. After looking at a text in its own context, however, we can turn back and see it again from the perspective of a later text or community. For example, there is reason to suppose that Isaiah 14 was originally written as a prediction of the downfall of the king of Assyria. We can interpret that text in light of the prophecy of eighth-century Isaiah of Jerusalem. About 150 years later, however, the Judean community in exile reinterpreted the passage so that it applied to the downfall of the king of Babylon in 538 BCE. The older context is primary to our interpretation, but the later context is also important in light of the first. Many centuries later, Christian readers of Isaiah connected the prophecy in Isaiah 14 to the story of Satan, the fallen angel. This created a

Conclusion

third context for interpretation, which takes its place in the historical sequence. So what is the passage "about"? It is about the king of Assyria, though the edited text says it's about the king of Babylon. Whichever king one identifies as the object of the prophecy, reading Satan in the text is clearly a later interpretation that is secondary to its original meaning.

The other possible direction is *backward*, that is, taking what we know to be true from later revelation and reading it back into the older text. This is essentially what Matthew does in his interpretation of the prophets. He knows that Jesus is the Messiah and that he was born of a virgin, so when the Greek text of Isaiah 7:14 mentions a virgin having a baby, it is perfectly natural for Matthew to identify this as a prophecy of Jesus. The same is true of Mark's identification of Jesus with the "son of man" in Daniel 7, the messiah who comes into power with God's apocalyptic victory over the powers of death and evil. For the crucified Jesus to be the Son of Man, however, one must interpret Daniel in an unusual way, taking into consideration many factors outside the apocalyptic tradition. This is why Jesus's identity as the Messiah is a secret in Mark until the crucifixion. Observers cannot possibly understand how Jesus fulfills Daniel 7 until they see him lifted up as king—on the cross.

So should one read only forward, being sure to avoid anachronism and external theological commitments? Or should one read only in reverse, finding the full meaning of the Old Testament in the light of the full revelation of Jesus? Within Christian communities each of these directions is essential for a full reading. Given what we discussed above about contexts and goals, however, it is clear that one need not read in both directions at all times or simultaneously. Sometimes it is more fitting to read forward, and other times a backward reading is appropriate and powerful. A Christian sermon about Isaiah 7, for example, might begin with a historical discussion of the eighth century BCE, showing how the passage represented hope for God's people in Judah. Then it might turn to a Christian reading that is guided by Matthew but that does not obliterate the historical significance of the text.

This kind of interpretation is difficult but needed within Christian communities. It enables a historically sensitive reading of the prophets that can be trampled in Christian interpretation. Furthermore, it allows Christians to understand better how their Christology arose and how it developed over time, alongside Jewish and other interpretations. One specific passage can bear the weight of several interpretations at once. Far from being a difficult or frightening idea, this is a liberating awareness. The word contained in the Bible is dynamic and alive, speaking within and through the variety of communities that engage it. The early Christians approached the prophets with a sense of excitement, freedom, and discovery, and we should as well, always in conversation with our community and traditions.

Finally, we should say a few words about the supposed contrast between the "Old Testament God" and the "New Testament God." It is common to hear that the Old Testament God is full of wrath and judgment while the New Testament God is full of mercy and grace. Hopefully our discussion of the prophets in this book has demonstrated how much the prophets are rooted in their hope for God's mercy and compassion. Jeremiah and other prophets suggest that God will not punish forever but will turn to redeem and restore the people, not because they deserve it or have said the right things but because mercy is more fundamental to the divine character than judgment. In fact, although the prophets certainly describe the punishment of God in harsh language, their purpose is to avoid the coming wrath or at least to show that God is not capricious or cruel, but just.

When Paul discusses God's gracious decision to open salvation to Jews and Gentiles in Romans 8–11, he is finally driven to exclaim the goodness and mystery of God's dealings with people: "O the depth of the riches and wisdom and knowledge of God! How unsearchable are his judgments and how inscrutable are his ways!" (Rom 11:33). This whole section—in which Paul develops a basic Christian understanding of

Conclusion

God—is rooted in the Old Testament. Paul and the other New Testament writers, and Jesus himself, affirm the essential continuity between the Hebrew scriptures and the revelation of Christ. Any biblical interpretation that drives a wedge between the testaments is one that does not attend carefully to the full tradition in both cases and that departs from the historical teachings of the church.

The challenge, then, is to understand the various voices that witness to God in the Bible. A primary conviction in the Old Testament is that God works in and through historical events, which means that the people involved in those events have a role in reporting them and interpreting their significance. From our later vantage point, we should determine what happened, how biblical writers understood those events, and how that understanding has been taken up and transformed by later interpreters. The unveiling of God's actions and purposes in history is a dynamic process that extends right through to contemporary readers. We should not dismiss the earliest stages of that process nor cast the ideas presented there in stone.

The Prophets: Past, Present, and Future

In this final section, we will consider a few issues related to contemporary interpretation of the prophets. In one sense, this whole book is an exercise in contemporary interpretation of the prophets. We are people living today, who know what we know, have our own questions, and try to understand the biblical prophets as best we can. In another sense, however, we have not directly addressed some of the major questions that modern readers must face in reading the prophets: Are they prophetic? Do they offer any prophetic word for today? If so, what is it?

First, the basic assumption in this study is that the prophets were historical figures who addressed their own social, political, and religious contexts. They spoke words that challenged, instructed, and encouraged the people to whom they were sent. God did not send the prophets to speak words that were unintelligible either to themselves or to their audience. God's message was not intended primarily or exclusively for "us," whichever "us" one has in mind.

It is interesting to observe how the prophets themselves deal with the problem of *near* future and *far* future. As we have seen, when they describe events in their immediate future, they use quite specific language. Isaiah mentions Ahaz and Rezin and Pekah by name in Isaiah 7, and his oracle is very precise about what will happen and when. On the other hand, when the prophets speak about events that are in the distant future, such as a time of salvation after the current crisis, their language becomes metaphorical and idealistic. Thus, Isaiah's prediction of God's salvation in Isaiah 2:1-4 describes the nations of the world streaming to Jerusalem and the end of all warfare and conflict. No specific ruler or timetable is mentioned, and the vision itself seems almost impossible to believe. In the prophets there is an interplay between a precise analysis of their own circumstances and an idealistic hope for a glorious time of redemption. The difference in time and scope is apparent in the language, style, and rhetoric of the various oracles.

Perhaps modern interpreters of the prophets can employ a similar technique in their reading. When the prophets speak specifically and directly about a situation, we can ask ourselves how that situation might apply specifically to our world and community. When the prophets speak generally and idealistically, we can let that language inspire our broader hope and confidence without tying it to any particular event or situation.

So what are the issues that the prophets tend to speak directly about? Economic injustice, judicial corruption, inept government, greed, jealousy, and religious apostasy. These social, political, and religious problems are everywhere and always. We can feel empowered by the prophets to speak directly against the powers of this world that oppress the weak, enrich themselves at the expense of the poor, and use their strength to advance themselves rather than to protect the vulnerable members of society.

Conclusion

Also, we should take care not to be like the audience in Jeremiah's temple sermon (Jer 7) who think that just because they dwell in the halls of power with God in their midst that they are innocent or safe. One of the major errors that the prophet's audience makes is when they assume the prophetic message is intended for someone else, that they are not under judgment because they currently live "at ease" and "in security." Perhaps we should not go on saying, "We are safe"—only to go on doing all these abominations (Jer 7:10). The temptation is to trust in the words of our tradition without truly engaging those ideas in a critical, self-reflective way. Like Jeremiah's listeners, we are tempted either to ignore the deeper meanings that emerge from the text or to crystalize one particular interpretation that serves our current interests. As we have seen, the prophetic tradition is dynamic and imaginative, and our own process of analyzing the present and envisioning the future should be as lively and dialogical as that of the prophets themselves.

Our application of the prophets to our world should first seek to bring their message of God's justice and righteousness to bear on our world and community. But what about the future aspects of the prophets' predictions regarding judgment and salvation? As we discussed in the "History and Theology" section, it would be problematic to simply transfer the prophets' predictions of violent destruction to our own world. The biblical tradition as a whole and the developing theology of God will not bear such a direct application. Those predictions of coming destruction, however, are not irrelevant. One central affirmation of the prophets is that much of the nation's suffering is self-inflicted. They have pursued ill-advised alliances with foreign powers and established an economic system that is essentially exploitative. When they are invaded by those same foreign powers or their economic system leads to the degradation of society, they can blame only themselves. It is possible to talk about the laws of cause and effect, even punishment and reward, without assigning particular catastrophic events to God's direct intervention. The same is true of the images of the environmental degradation (e.g., Jer 9:10) that is the inevitable result of military invasion. These visions of judgment are as applicable to our world as ever.

The second aspect of the prophets' vision of the future is the eschatological time of redemption, peace, and reconciliation. This message of hope and comfort is absolutely relevant to our time. The people are invited to look beyond the current time of difficulty to see a larger divine plan unfolding. This hope gives them the strength to hold on during trials and the faith to remain true to God despite hardships. It is also essential to remember that this hopeful prophetic voice is not a heavenly vision. The people are not asked to keep their head down, stay passive, and wait for blessings in heaven. Repeatedly the prophets suggest that if the people turn back to God, then God will turn back to them. Isaiah says that if the people truly honor the requirements of the covenant—especially in the way they feed the hungry, clothe the naked, and honor the Sabbath—that God will heal the people and transform their community (Isa 58). This positive hope of salvation is an encouragement to live in covenantal community with God and with each other, not a reason to disengage from the world. In this, the prophetic hope of salvation is as applicable to our world as ever.

www.ingramcontent.com/pod-product-compliance
Lightning Source LLC
Chambersburg PA
CBHW060518100426
42743CB00009B/1361